How Karma Works

*The Twelve Links
of Dependent Arising*

HOW KARMA WORKS

The Twelve Links of Dependent Arising

An Oral Teaching by
Geshe Sonam Rinchen

Translated and edited by Ruth Sonam

Snow Lion Publications
Ithaca, New York
Boulder, Colorado

Snow Lion Publications
P.O. Box 6483
Ithaca, New York 14851   USA
607-273-8519
www.snowlionpub.com

Printed in Canada on acid-free, recycled paper.

ISBN-13: 978-1-55939-254-9
ISBN-10: 1-55939-254-1

Library of Congress Cataloging-in-Publication Data

Sonam Rinchen, 1933-
    How karma works : the twelve links of dependent arising / an oral teaching by Geshe Sonam Rinchen ; translated and edited by Ruth Sonam.
        p. cm.
    Included is a complete translation of Chapter 26 from Nagarjuna's Fundamental Treatise on the Middle Way (Mulamadhyamikakarika). "The root text: Examining the twelve links of existence."
    Includes bibliographical references.
    ISBN-13: 978-1-55939-254-9 (alk. paper)
    ISBN-10: 1-55939-254-1 (alk. paper)
    1. Pratītyasamutpāda. 2. Karma. 3. Nāgārjuna, 2nd cent. Madhyamakakārikā. I. Sonam, Ruth, 1943- . II. Nāgārjuna, 2nd cent. Madhyamakakārikā. English. Selections. III. Tsoṅ-kha-pa Blo-bzaṅ-grags-pa, 1357-1419. Rtsa śes tik chen rigs pa'i rgya mtsho. IV. Title.
BQ4240.S67 2006
294.3'422—DC22
                                                                2006011304

CONTENTS

ACKNOWLEDGMENT

The author and translator would like to thank their editor Susan Kyser for her invaluable assistance.

1 THE WHEEL OF EXISTENCE

The Buddha's supreme disciples Shariputra and Maudgal-yayana are said to have visited various otherworldly realms, including the hell realms. On their return they described six states of existence to the Buddha's followers and spoke about the four noble truths, explaining the process of taking rebirth in a way that made a profound impact on their listeners. The Buddha knew that they would not always be present to do this, so he arranged for images depicting this process—the twelve links of dependent arising—to be painted in the porches of temples. In each temple a monk was given the task of explaining these paintings and their import to those who were interested. Even today many Tibetan temples contain an image of the wheel of existence painted on the walls at the entrance.

In this depiction, the twelve links are shown as part of the wheel or circle of existence, which is held by the Lord of Death, who appears as an ogre. He grips the wheel with the long claws of his front and hind paws, holding it against his belly and chest. The top of the wheel is in his mouth. At the hub are three creatures: a pig, a bird, and a snake, denoting ignorance, desire, and anger, respectively. They are at the center of the wheel because these three main disturbing

Wheel of Existence. Drawing by Amdo Jamyang.

emotions are the primary causes that keep us in cyclic existence. The snake and the bird seem to be coming out of the pig's mouth because ignorance is the principal of these three disturbing states of mind.

The wheel is divided into sections of which the three lower ones show the realms of hell beings, hungry spirits, and animals. These segments signify the suffering of pain. There are three upper sections representing the human realm, the abodes of the gods belonging to the desire realm, and those of the gods belonging to the form realm. The first two represent the suffering of change, while the latter represents the pervasive suffering of conditioning.

The different kinds of suffering have been caused by contaminated actions underlain by the disturbing emotions. To show how this happens, the twelve links of dependent arising—ignorance, formative action, consciousness, name and form, the six sources, contact, feeling, craving, grasping, existence, birth, and aging and death—are painted around the rim of the wheel.[1]

The scenes within each section show what living beings experience in that particular kind of rebirth. The fact that the Lord of Death holds the wheel of existence in his mouth signifies impermanence and that everything is subject to transience. Up above is the moon, symbolizing the third noble truth, true cessation of suffering. Below that is the Buddha pointing to this moon to remind us that he has shown us the path to liberation and has taught the four truths in an unerring way. His presence is a sign that we cannot reach freedom without understanding what needs to be practiced and what must be avoided. For this we depend on him and our spiritual teachers, who communicate to us what he taught. At the bottom of the painting there are usually some lines explaining the process that keeps us in cyclic existence and how that process can be reversed. These lines indicate the key insights that we need to gain while we practice the fourth noble truth, the true paths.

In paintings of the wheel of existence certain images are traditionally used to symbolize each of the twelve links, though these may vary. (1) The initial ignorance that starts the whole process off each time is shown as a blind old woman. She is not only unable to see what lies before her but wanders around lost. This illustrates how our inability to understand reality causes us to wander powerlessly through the three states of existence—the desire, form, and formless realms.[2]

(2) Formative action is a potter making pots and also sometimes the potter's wheel. The potter turns the wheel and produces different kinds of pots. Formative action is of different kinds—virtuous, nonvirtuous, and unfluctuating. These actions result in the different kinds of rebirth.

(3) Consciousness is a monkey in a house with six windows through which the monkey looks out. These windows symbolize our six faculties, through which we experience pleasure and pain.

(4) Name and form are a boat which conveys the idea of traveling from one life to another. This link is also sometimes represented by a tripod covered with cloth, like a shelter we might make on a hot day. The tripod cannot balance on two legs but needs all three to stand. The three are interdependent. Similarly the five aggregates that make up name and form are interdependent and cannot exist on their own. Moreover, the existence of the person depends on them. When we think about this, it helps us to understand lack of independence and to gain a correct understanding of reality—that things are empty of inherent existence and are all dependently existent.

(5) The six sources are an empty house or empty town. Sometimes from the outside a house appears to be inhabited,

but when we enter it, we realize it is empty. The empty house indicates that in the womb the different faculties gradually develop, but consciousness is not yet functioning in conjunction with them. The mental faculty is present from the outset, but the other five faculties develop as the fetus grows. They are unable to experience their objects until the link of contact occurs. The empty house also stands for selflessness. The six faculties come into being through the force of past actions, but they are not the objects of use or possessions of an intrinsically existent self.

(6) Contact is a couple engaged in sexual union. To have intercourse their bodies must touch. For contact to occur, an object of perception, a faculty, and a consciousness must come together.

(7) Feeling is a person whose eye is pierced by an arrow. Just as we would feel intense pain the moment that happened, so when the quality of an object is discerned, pleasurable, painful, or neutral sensations or feelings immediately follow.

(8) Craving is a person drinking beer. Alcoholics never feel satisfied no matter how much they drink. On the contrary, their craving for alcohol simply increases. They will drink away their wealth, property, and possessions. Similarly desire keeps growing. We crave different kinds of feelings and wish not to be separated from pleasurable ones, to be free from unpleasant and painful ones as quickly as possible, and for neutral feelings not to decline. Craving keeps growing and makes us perform all kinds of negative actions that bring us suffering.

(9) Grasping is a monkey sitting in a tree full of ripe fruit. While it eats one fruit, it is already reaching out to take another. It is consumed by greed and cannot be satisfied. Grasping is reaching out for the aggregates of the next life.

(10) Existence is a woman who is nine months pregnant

and whose baby is fully grown in the womb, about to be born. Existence occurs when the imprint of a former action has been fully activated through craving and grasping and everything is ready to produce the next rebirth.

(11) Birth is a woman holding her newly born child, while (12) aging and death are shown as someone who is no longer young carrying a corpse.

The usual way in which the twelve links are enumerated, which emphasizes the relationships between the links, differs from the order in which they actually occur. The first three links begin the process. Then the eighth, ninth, and tenth occur, followed by the fourth, fifth, sixth, and seventh. The eleventh occurs simultaneously with the fourth and marks the point of conception. Regarding the twelfth link, aging begins the moment after conception and thus inevitably precedes death.

Most of us have not done much philosophical speculation about our own origins or those of the world but we do hold some hazy ideas about what is responsible for our experiences of suffering or happiness. Usually we attribute them to external factors and circumstances or we may go a little beyond our everyday material world and attribute them to spirit influences, the phases of the moon, the astrological position of constellations, and so forth. Many people regard misfortune as some kind of punishment. The Buddha encouraged us to look within and think more deeply about what is responsible for our present condition. He pointed out that as long as we continue to be born as a result of our ignorance and the compulsive actions which stem from it, we cannot escape the many kinds of physical and mental suffering that are their inevitable consequence.

2 THE ROOT OF OUR TROUBLES

The Buddha taught many different practices which form the
paths and stages that enable us to accomplish the goal of
spiritual life—a good rebirth, liberation from cyclic existence, or complete enlightenment. All of these practices and
their results are for the purpose of removing the troubles of
the world. "The world," used to translate the Tibetan term
jigten (*'jig rten*), here has a very specific meaning because
it refers to the five aggregates—forms, feelings, discriminations, compositional factors, and the six kinds of consciousness[3]—which constitute our own and others' bodies and
minds. The person or self depends on these five aggregates,
and it is in relation to them that we come into existence and
disintegrate. Thus "basis of disintegration" is one meaning for *jigten*. Those who are born again and again in the
six different states of cyclic existence, repeatedly taking on
now bodies and relinquishing them life after life, are called
worldly beings. Animals are considered to be in a bad state
of rebirth, while humans are in a good state because they
experience greater happiness, their suffering is less intense,
and they are able to do what is necessary to insure their future well-being.

The troubles of the world refer to birth, sickness, aging and death, not getting what we want, getting what we

don't want, and seeking but not finding. They are the consequences of having taken birth with this kind of body and mind, the product of past actions underlain by the disturbing emotions. In this sense the body and mind are said to be contaminated. They are the basis for all our present suffering and in addition act like a magnet, attracting future suffering as well.

Every action leaves its imprint on the mind, and later craving and grasping activate the imprint to bring about its result. Underlying this kind of action is our ignorance, namely our innate misconception of the self, the root of all our troubles. The only way to rid ourselves of this misconception is to understand how the self actually exists, which is diametrically opposed to how that misconception perceives it.

The person and all other existent phenomena are dependently existent. Whatever is produced depends on the causes and conditions that produce it. All phenomena are dependent on their parts as well as on a valid basis of attribution and the process of attribution. The understanding of this allows us to realize that things could not possibly be independent as they appear to be. Nothing at all has even the slightest degree of true intrinsic existence. Everything exists in dependence on other factors and is thus free from the two extremes: the extreme of reified objective existence and the extreme of complete nonexistence.

Lack of inherent existence is not equivalent to nonexistence, and we must train ourselves to distinguish between these two. Emptiness implies that things are dependent. Since anything produced depends on causes and conditions, the causes and conditions we ourselves create through our thoughts and actions are of seminal importance. The principal cause that allows us to overcome our cyclic existence and the basic misconception that underlies it is familiarizing ourselves with emptiness and the dependently existent nature of things.

There is a difference between doing this by employing limited lines of reasoning and by using a multitude of approaches to establish that things exist in a middle way between objective existence and complete nonexistence. Whether this familiarization takes place for only a short time or over a long period also makes a difference. Whether or not this practice is accompanied by the creation of abundant positive energy or merit influences the outcome too. These various factors determine what kind of result is accomplished.

By using a restricted approach for a limited period and supporting this with a moderate accumulation of positive energy, we can gain freedom from the disturbing attitudes and emotions as well as their seeds, but not more. On the other hand, when we employ many different lines of reasoning again and again for a long time and create substantial merit, the force of our understanding will remove even the subtlest imprints of the disturbing attitudes and emotions.

Usually emptiness is explained in relation to the great classical Mahayana[4] texts, such as Nagarjuna's *Treatise on the Middle Way*,[5] Chandrakirti's *Supplement to the Middle Way*,[6] or Shantideva's *Way of the Bodhisattva*,[7] which elucidate how Bodhisattvas meditate on emptiness. Investigating the nature of reality in this way is challenging and requires courage because we need breadth of perspective and a willingness to explore. If we want something quick and easy, this will prove too demanding. But we should remember that even in everyday life it frequently pays to go into greater depth.

Along with the breadth of outlook we need the plentiful positive energy created through love, compassion, and the spirit of enlightenment[8] and through the practice of the six perfections.[9] We should not think that the understanding of reality can be separated from these attitudes and conduct. Insight and skillful means must always be combined.

As intelligent people we must look for the very heart of Buddhist practice and investigate how this relates to our minds and whether it is relevant to our lives. If it is, we need to gain a good understanding of it and then apply what we have learned, continually deepening our understanding and practice. Setting out for a destination with reliable and detailed instructions for getting there is very different from setting out without any clear idea of where one is going.

As long as we see the teachings as somehow distinct from our lives, we have failed to understand them properly. Most of us can devote at most an hour or two each day to formal practice. Regarding only this as true practice and the rest of our day as something quite separate will severely restrict what we can do in our lifetime. But if practice becomes part of our daily life, we can use the many opportunities that present themselves to work at transforming our attitudes and emotional responses in a positive way.

For some of us a quarter of our life has passed. For others half our life or more is already over, and maybe we are closer to death than we think. How much of that time have we devoted to becoming more kindhearted and to thinking and living in a more constructive way? We need to look honestly at ourselves and see how much sincere effort we have made. If, since encountering the teachings, we haven't really tried to change, it is absurd to complain that the teachings haven't helped us and aren't effective. For most of us our practice of the teachings and our endeavor to bring about inner change remain of secondary importance. But they need to become our foremost concern. Educated people can understand the teachings, but understanding alone cannot bring about transformation. In fact the knowledge we gain may easily be used for other purposes.

Most of us want to be thought of as wise and kindhearted human beings. To become like that takes conscious effort.

Kindheartedness is the fulcrum for all development within the Great Vehicle. Nowadays, because people lack sufficient genuine interest, it is becoming difficult to find those who are really receptive to these teachings. But thinking about the principal themes of the Great Vehicle, such as love and compassion, for even a few minutes is time well spent. If a moment of anger can be extremely destructive, it is equally true that a moment of heartfelt love or compassion can be tremendously constructive.

3 DEPENDENT ARISING

If things were not empty of inherent existence, nothing could function and neither actions nor the agents of those actions would be feasible. It is their emptiness of inherent existence that allows everything to operate satisfactorily. When we understand the dependently arising nature of things properly, we will also understand the four noble truths: suffering, the sources of suffering, the cessation of suffering, and the paths of insight that lead to this freedom from suffering. So dependent arising is crucial.

We first need to know what dependent arising or dependent existence means in general. The Tibetan expression *ten ching drel war jung wa* (*rten cing 'brel bar 'byung ba*) is used as a translation of the Sanskrit *prafītyasamutpāda*. In English the words "arising" or "origination" are often used to translate the Tibetan *jung wa* (*'byung ba*). This can be misleading because it seems to refer to an event or occurrence with implications that something is produced, but this is not necessarily so. "Dependent arising" refers to dependence on causes and conditions but also to dependence on parts and on attribution. Everything that exists is dependently existent. If anything exists, it does so dependently.

When we think about the spiritual traditions in which we have been brought up, does this idea fit comfortably with them? Or do we believe there is something that does not rely on other factors but is independent? In fact this emphasis on the dependent nature of everything that exists is unique to the Buddha's teachings. There have been many excellent teachers who have said many excellent and helpful things, but the Buddha is praised as an incomparable teacher because of his unsurpassable explanation of reality in terms of dependent existence.

There are two kinds of dependently arising phenomena—products and non-products. Products fit into one of two categories—they are either with or without form. Those with form are easier to identify than those without. Science is mainly concerned with investigating what, from a Buddhist point of view, is form in varying degrees of subtlety. Products without form are different kinds of awareness and non-associated compositional factors, namely those things that are neither awareness nor matter, such as persons, time, birth, aging, duration, and impermanence.[10]

Some assert that when we reach a very subtle level of these products, for instance particles or infinitesimal moments of time, there exist things that are functional inasmuch as they are produced by causes and conditions and themselves produce results, which are nevertheless unchanging. But could such things actually exist? If anything is a product and produces other phenomena, it must undergo change itself.

It is difficult for us to conceive of anything that is unchanging. Is anything that we perceive through our five senses unchanging? If not, then permanent or unchanging phenomena must appear to the sixth kind of awareness, mental consciousness, and mainly to conceptual awareness. Shut your eyes and think of your home, of something in your home or of someone close to you. An image appears. To what kind of awareness does it appear? Not to visual or auditory perception but to mental awareness. Does the image that appears in this way undergo change or not? Perhaps you left a book on the left side of the table in your room. In the meantime someone has moved it, but the image of the book on the left side of the table still appears to your mind. It is considered to be a non-product since it does not undergo change moment by moment. Mental images constantly appear to us, so it's worth exploring what kind of phenomena they are.

In the twenty-fourth chapter of his *Treatise on the Middle Way*, Nagarjuna says:

> Whatever arises dependently
> Is explained as empty.
> Thus dependent attribution
> Is the middle way.

> Since there is nothing whatever
> That is not dependently existent,
> For that reason there is nothing
> Whatsoever that is not empty.[11]

Here Nagarjuna states the Madhyamika or middle way position. Everything that exists does so dependently and everything that is dependently existent necessarily lacks independent objective existence.

What are dependently arising non-products? They are phenomena that do not come into existence through causes and conditions and thus do not undergo constant change. They are dependent on parts and on attribution.

Emptiness or lack of true existence is a non-product because it does not come into being through causes and conditions and does not undergo change. Emptiness is the fundamental nature of anything that exists but is nevertheless also dependently existent because, for instance, it depends on the phenomenon whose fundamental nature it is. It is difficult for us to gain a clear concept of non-products since they are more subtle than the things that appear to our sense perceptions. It is essential, however, to understand that both products and non-products are dependently existent.

4 How Things Are Produced

Products come into existence through causes and conditions. Asanga in his *Compendium of Knowledge*[12] mentions three conditions in this context: the condition of no movement; the condition of impermanence; and the condition of potential. The *Rice Seedling Sutra* says: "Because this exists, that occurs" which indicates the condition of no movement. "Because this has been produced, that has been produced" indicates the condition of impermanence. "Conditioned by ignorance there is formative action" refers to the condition of potential.[13]

Many hold firmly to a belief that products, namely the physical world (often termed the container) and the living beings in it (referred to as the contents), come into existence through some creative force, such as Brahma, Indra, Vishnu or another creator, and that the act of creation is preceded by an intention. To negate that the physical world and living beings have been created in this way, Buddhist scholars place emphasis on the fact that every product comes into existence in dependence on its own specific causes and conditions and not through the intention of a creator god. This aspect of production is called the condition of no movement because there is no movement of intention involved.

Discourse on dependent arising constitutes discussion of a philosophical view, in this case the cornerstone of Buddhist philosophy. When we consider how things actually exist, which is what philosophy is about, it is important not to be prejudiced in favor of our own views but to be openminded and honest, and to conduct our investigation intelligently with enthusiasm to discover the nature of reality. If we hold certain beliefs, our tendency is to avoid anything that threatens them. Our principal concern should be to discover how things actually are and then build on that.

"Because this has been produced, that has been produced" refers to the condition of impermanence and counters the belief that our world and living beings have been created by a force which is permanent. This force may be identified as a god or as some other creative principle which is unchanging and eternal. From a Buddhist point of view a condition, which here acts as a cause, is itself something produced by its own specific causes and conditions. It ceases when its result comes into existence. If an unchanging producer of things existed, it should either constantly produce without ever stopping or it should never produce anything at all because it could not undergo change from a state of production to one of no production. The container and the contents have not come from any cause or condition of this kind.

Others believe that the world and living beings have come about causelessly or have arisen from causes that are actually incompatible. A thing can only arise from concordant or compatible causes, which are those that have the potential to produce the particular result. For instance, in the context of the twelve-part process, ignorance gives rise to formative action. The compulsive contaminated actions that keep us in cyclic existence can only come from causes that possess the potential to produce them, namely from disturbing attitudes and emotions. The understanding of reality will never produce such actions. Thus things come into existence from their own specific causes and conditions, from that which is impermanent and compatible. No products, whether external, meaning not connected to our mental continuum, or internal, meaning connected to our mental continuum, come into existence through a creative force that formulates an intention to create them, from a permanent and unchanging principle, causelessly, or from discordant causes.

For instance, does a sunflower seed embody all three of the conditions we have mentioned? It is a condition of no movement for the sunflower because it does not formulate any intention to create a sunflower nor is there any force at work which intends the seed to create the sunflower.

The sunflower seed is an impermanent condition because it itself came into existence through other causes and conditions. At the moment when it ceases, its result, the sunflower seedling, appears. The sunflower seed is a condition with potential because it has the specific capacity to produce a sunflower—something that is related to it—and will not produce any other kind of flower. The presence of a healthy sunflower seed and the other essential conditions will produce a sunflower. It will not come into existence without the presence of that seed nor will a zinnia seed produce a sunflower. So the sunflower does not come into being causelessly nor from discordant causes.

Similarly ignorance, the first of the twelve links, is a condition embodying all three conditions of no movement, of impermanence, and of potential. It produces formative action, the second link, which, in turn, acts as all three factors in the production of the third link, consciousness.

When we think about how things come into existence, not in terms of the sunflower and its seed but in relation to our own experience of happiness and suffering, we realize that suffering is not inflicted on us by some other force, but that it is a product, a natural outcome and result of certain conditions, as is the sunflower.

Pleasure and pain, happiness and suffering are the result of the three conditions mentioned above. They do not occur through the impetus of a creator who intends us to have these experiences, are not created by any force which is itself permanent, nor do they occur randomly or as a result of discordant causes. If we want to experience more happiness and less suffering, we must change what we think and do. We can create causes and conditions with the power to produce happiness and avoid doing what will bring us suffering. If our experiences were the result of some creator's will, we could only turn to that creator and pray. However, from the Buddhist perspective, the responsibility lies with us.

The *Rice Seedling Sutra* explains that all dependently arising products, whether external or internal, have five features.[14] These five, like the three conditions mentioned above, negate certain beliefs. The first feature is that products come into existence through causes and conditions, which demonstrates that they do not arise causelessly. The second feature is that they come into existence through a diversity of impermanent conditions. This shows that they cannot be the result of a single cause which is eternal, unchanging, and indivisible. A seedling has not come into existence causelessly, because it depends on its main cause, the seed, as well as on a variety of cooperative conditions, such as moisture, temperature, the growing medium, and other factors.

The third feature is that every product has come into existence from causes which are themselves selfless. There are those who hold that our six faculties and their objects are a truly existent "I" and "mine." To counter this view it is stressed that the five sense faculties and our mental faculty, referred to as internal sources, and the six external sources, namely sights, sounds, smells, tastes, and tactile sensations, which are the five objects of the senses, and the objects of the mental faculty, have all been produced by causes and conditions that lack independent existence and so lack any truly existent self. Ordinary people regard the senses as a real self and the objects of the senses as objects of use or experience by such a self. Of course, there is a person or "I" who experiences but that person or self does not exist as it appears to do. Nor do the objects we experience through our senses exist objectively as they seem to do.

The fourth feature is that these products arise from causes and conditions that have the potential to produce them. This resembles the third of the three conditions mentioned above. The fifth is that they arise through lack of activity, which is equivalent to the first of the three conditions, the condition of no movement. Emphasis on these conditions and features is intended to help us overcome false beliefs we may have about how things are produced and exist. The *Rice Seedling Sutra* says: "If you ask why they are said to be dependently existent, it is because they have causes and they have conditions and are not without causes and conditions."[15]

All of us can understand the more obvious aspects of how a seed produces a seedling and that this requires the presence of the main cause and a number of contributing factors. The seed ceases and the sprout comes into existence without any hiatus in this process. But how do we come into existence, since each one of us is also a product? The production of a seedling from a seed is not as simple as it appears, though rather less complex than our own production. Are we the same substantial continuum as the ignorance that has produced us and is it our main or special cause? We cannot be one substantial continuum with the ignorance responsible for our present rebirth because we would have to be awareness and a mental factor, since ignorance is a type of awareness and a mental factor or activity.

The sperm and ovum of our parents are the main cause for our body of this life and are cooperative causes for the person we are, just as the tools used by a carpenter to make a table are contributing or cooperative causes.

Taking the example of a child: has this child been produced from a cause which is a condition of no movement? Has there been a movement of intention to create it? What about a planned pregnancy? And what about the carpenter's intention to make the table? An architect draws a plan and then a building is constructed. Did the building come into existence through a movement of intention? We would probably say that mountains, valleys, and rivers are not the outcome of creative effort, but that houses, pots, tables, and persons are. If some products come into being through a movement of intention while others do not, we cannot make the general statement that products do not come into existence through the movement of intention.

In this context a movement of intention refers specifically to an intention formulated by a creator, such as the gods Brahma, Indra, Vishnu, or Ishvara in the Hindu pantheon. Are the things mentioned above created by them, and if they are, is the creative effort made by such a creator the outcome of a movement of intention? According to the Buddhist point of view there is no such creator nor any creation of this kind.

In the twelve-part process is formative action, the second part, the result of a movement of the mind? Who or what creates that formative action? We create and accumulate the action. Doesn't it occur through a movement of intention? We hear again and again in the Buddhist teachings that there is no external creator, but that everything has come into existence through our actions, which originate in our minds.

Our minds are, therefore, the sole creator. I have raised these points to show how much there is to think about.

Those who believe that everything is produced by a creator do not discount the role played by the seed but assert that the basic nature of the seed and that of the seedling are the same and that both are of the same nature as the creator. The creation is seen as an aspect or manifestation of the creator. This is a highly simplified presentation of certain beliefs associated with a creator, and it is worth investigating the sophisticated philosophical systems that underlie such assertions.

According to the *Rice Seedling Sutra* dependently arising products are profound in five ways. They are profound from the point of view of their causes, because they have not arisen causelessly nor have they been produced by a self that is a separate entity and a creator. They are profound as regards their nature or character, because they do not act as a separate self-existent creative force. They are profound in relation to their mode of production, because though they depend on many factors, they come into existence from their own specific causes and conditions without any confusion, and those factors have not created them with any prior intention of doing so. They are profound with respect to their duration, because they appear to exist for a protracted period even though they disintegrate moment by moment. They are profound in regard to their origins, because they come into existence through causes, but when an investigation is made to ascertain whether they come into existence from that which is of the same nature, that which is of a different nature, that which is both of the former, or whether they come into existence causelessly, they are difficult to understand.

When we investigate the natural world, ourselves, and the objects which surround us, we find there are other aspects of dependently arising products that may also be discussed:

how they are not unchanging; how they do not discontinue; how a cause cannot produce a result without undergoing some change; how a small cause, such as an apple seed, can produce a significant result, such as a large fruit-bearing tree; how products are the outcome of a continuum. If we can establish the basis correctly, namely what actually exists and how it exists, we will also be able to establish proper paths of practice, which must be based on reality.

Do non-Buddhist philosophical systems accept dependent existence? And how do Buddhist philosophical systems view dependent existence? Everyone, of course, agrees that seedlings come from seeds, but when we investigate more closely, we are forced to consider the seedling's actual nature. Is its nature the same as that of the seed? What is its true identity?

As has been said, the basic premise from the Prasangika point of view is that things exist dependently and are empty of intrinsic existence. Because of being empty in this way, their existence is necessarily a dependent one. This is emphasized to bring home to us that there is no self of persons or of other phenomena. Even though they lack such a self or identity and have no independent or objective existence from their own side, because they exist depending on a diversity of factors, they do indisputably exist. What is affirmed is their selflessness, and what is negated is that they come into existence through a permanent, unchanging creative force, that they have arisen causelessly, and that they have arisen from discordant causes.

Non-Buddhist Indian schools of philosophy generally do not accept that everything is dependently existent and assert that all phenomena are truly existent. The great Tibetan master Je Tsongkhapa[16] writes that these assertions are not inconsistent nor anything to be ashamed of, since they are following the tenets of their own philosophical systems. He goes on to say that the Vaibhashikas, Sautrantikas and Chittamatrins,[17] who are proponents of Buddhist systems of thought, accept the dependent arising of things produced from causes and conditions but nevertheless assert that these things are truly existent. This, he says, is an absurd contradiction. If one were to say to them that things are not truly existent because they arise in dependence on causes and conditions, they would dismiss this, since for them the very fact of their dependent arising confirms their true existence.

All proponents of Buddhist philosophical tenets accept the dependent arising of produced things. However, dependent arising defined by dependence on parts is not generally accepted by the lower schools of Buddhist philosophy. The Vaibhashikas and Sautrantikas assert the existence of partless functional things,[18] such as partless particles and moments of awareness. Those things could not, in that case, depend on their parts. The Madhyamikas assert that all products and non-products depend on their parts.

There are three Tibetan terms with a similar meaning: *tenpa (rten pa),* to depend; *drepa ('phrad pa),* to meet; and *töpa (ltos pa),* to be related. In this context they are associated with the Tibetan expression for arising in dependence *teney jung wa (rten nas byung ba)* or its longer form, meaning arising in dependence and relationship, *ten ching drel war jung wa (rten cing 'brel bar 'byung ba),* mentioned earlier. So when, in reference to dependently arising products, *jung wa* has the sense of produced, we can say arising or produced in dependence, through meeting, and through relationship.[19] But *jung wa,* as we have already seen, can also mean existing, and so when we say arising or existing in dependence, through meeting, and through relationship, this refers to the dependently existent nature of all things, both products and non-products.[20]

Now do these three—arising in dependence, through meeting, and through relationship—actually mean the same thing? For instance, the seedling has come into existence in dependence upon and in relation to the seed and to heat, moisture, and a growing medium. If something has arisen dependently, does it follow that it has also arisen through meeting? Does it need to meet what it depends upon? Have we come into being in dependence upon the person we were in our last life? Has the person of this life met with the person of the last life? For instance, if we were a god in our last life, have we met with that god? On the other hand meeting does not necessarily involve dependence because a tiger and the deer it kills have met but the two are not in a relationship of dependence. The three terms are similar but not completely synonymous in this context.

In his *Compendium of Knowledge* Asanga lists eleven points about dependent arising with respect to products: they do not have a creator whose self is a separate entity from the aggregates; they have causes; they are not objects used by self-sufficient substantially existent living beings; they are under the influence of other factors; they come into existence with no movement of intention; they are impermanent; they are momentary because they come in a continuum of many moments of a similar type; they are part of an unbroken continuity of causes and effects; there is concordance between causes and effects; there is a diversity of causes and effects; there are specific and definite causes and effects.[21]

These eleven points demonstrate impermanence, suffering, and, in a general way, emptiness and selflessness. The first, that products are not created by a self which is a separate entity from the aggregates, indicates their emptiness of and lack of relationship to such an eternal, unitary, independent self. The third, that they are not objects of use by a substantially existent self-sufficient person, similarly indicates their lack of such a self.

The last three points show that dependently arising products associated with cyclic existence are unsatisfactory by nature because they correspond to their causes which are contaminated actions and disturbing attitudes and emotions. They arise in multifarious forms through the influence of these and take these particular forms as a result of specific causes and conditions. The other facts all demonstrate their impermanence.

As we have seen, products can be divided into external and internal products. Living beings and the five aggregates that make up their bodies and minds are internal products. Those that are not connected to consciousness, namely the physical environment consisting of mountains, lakes, rivers, and so forth, are produced from their own particular causes and conditions and are external products.

Why are dependently arising products divided into these two categories? Understanding the dependently arising nature of internal products helps us to stop seeing them as a truly existent self, while understanding that external products are dependently existent enables us to overcome the conception of them as inherently existent objects of experience by an inherently existent self.

Dependently arising phenomena are also classified as belonging either to the afflicted side, referring to everything associated with cyclic existence, or to the purified side, which refers to nirvana or the state beyond sorrow and the ending of worldly existence.[22] This is to help us overcome our clinging to true existence by emphasizing that neither the afflicted side, of which we need to rid ourselves, nor the purified side, consisting of what needs to be adopted and cultivated, is inherently existent.

Dependently arising phenomena of the afflicted side can be summarized as true sources of suffering and their outcome, true suffering. When this is expanded, it can be presented in terms of the twelve-part process of dependent arising by which we remain in cyclic existence. Dependently arising phenomena of the purified side consist of true cessation and true paths of insight. When these are expanded upon, we consider how stopping ignorance stops all the other aspects of the twelve-part process, and how this is the way that we can extricate ourselves from cyclic existence.

5 Extricating Ourselves

In the *Rice Seedling Sutra* the Buddha clearly indicated the dependent nature of things and the process which keeps us in cyclic existence with the words, "Conditioned by ignorance there is formative action." How do we remain in cyclic existence and how can we extricate ourselves?

By meditating on the twelve links, we can come to understand fully how painful our present situation actually is. This is something we are reluctant to acknowledge, but a real antipathy towards the cycle of involuntary birth and death in which we are trapped will not arise unless we face it. And unless we generate strong feelings of aversion to cyclic existence, it will be impossible to develop a genuine wish for liberation, without which progress on the path is impossible. Yet revulsion for cyclic existence is still not enough. Unless we recognize what keeps us in this condition, we cannot discover the means to free ourselves. Even though we may realize that we are sick, unless a correct diagnosis is made, we cannot hope to find the treatment that can cure us.

We begin by thinking about our impending death and retracing the steps that lead to it. This is called contemplating the afflicted side of the twelve links in reverse order. Through this we realize that the nature of cyclic existence is painful. It will make us want to change our condition and stimulates the aspiration for freedom. In this case it is of no benefit to think about others and their predicament. We must look at our own situation. Having been born, we will inevitably have to face death. We are on our deathbed full of grief and distress at leaving this world. Our bodily functions are ceasing, which causes us physical suffering in addition to the anguish we feel. The mental and physical suffering we experience stirs up all kinds of delusions.

This more or less describes the general and clearly apparent experience of death. Surely it is the greatest physical and mental crisis that we will have to face in this life. If we do not think so, it's probably because we have never given death much thought.

When we examine from where all the grief, distress, and physical suffering come, we discover that it is a result of aging and sickness and ultimately of birth itself. Birth is the outcome of our compulsive actions, which spring from ignorance. So, when we contemplate the process of the twelve links in reverse order in this way, we begin with the outright suffering experienced as we are dying and retrace the causes back to ignorance, the root of our cyclic existence and of our misery. Whether we continue to wander through the different states of cyclic existence or whether we extricate ourselves from this condition depends upon whether or not we deal with that basic ignorance, our own misconception of the self. Reaching a point where we can fully recognize this is a substantial accomplishment.

There are two ways of meditating on the twelve-part process—from the conventional and ultimate points of view. The conventional entails contemplating the afflicted and purified aspects of the twelve links in forward and reverse sequence.[23] The ultimate consists of meditating on the emptiness of each of the individual links and of the whole process. It is important to meditate on both of these aspects because if we only meditate on the ultimate aspect, we are in danger of falling into a nihilist view, which is to believe that nothing has any actual existence. On the other hand, by only meditating on the conventional aspects of the process we may fall into the other extreme and make it all much more concrete than it really is. We must steer the middle path between seeing things as completely nonexistent and seeing them as objectively existent.

To turn now to the process of the twelve links in forward sequence, described in the *Rice Seedling Sutra*: first there is ignorance, which is a basic confusion that gives rise to distorted perception and leads to certain kinds of action. Thus ignorance is the first link and formative action, the second. The action ceases but leaves an imprint in the mind, which is indicated by the third link, consciousness. Just before death, craving and grasping, the eighth and ninth links, activate that imprint and lead to conception and the development in the womb of the senses and the ability to experience. Birth then takes place and everything begins again. Every moment of ignorance that leads to formative action begins another set of twelve links, so there are, in fact, many sets operating simultaneously. Intelligent scrutiny reveals both what an exhausting, self-perpetuating process it is and how we can get rid of it.

The basic confusion or misconception is primarily a certain way of seeing the self. We have to examine whether this way of seeing the self is valid or mistaken. You see something on the hill opposite but are not sure whether it's a human being or a scarecrow. The closer you go, the more clearly you see that it's a human being. Now you can be sure that your perception of it as a human being is correct. If, on the other hand, you feel uncertain about what is there but think it might be a human being when in fact it is a scarecrow, the closer you get the more indistinct your perception of it as a human being becomes and the more clearly you see it as a scarecrow. The perception of what is actually there stops the misperception.

When a perception accords with fact, the more we investigate the clearer it becomes, whereas when what we perceive does not accord with fact, careful investigation will reveal our mistake. We recognize that what our perception clings to is a mere fabrication, something which doesn't exist at all. This applies to our ignorance. The more familiar we become with how things actually exist, the weaker our misperception grows until it stops altogether. Although the misconception does not stop right away, the more we accustom ourselves to seeing things as they actually are, the weaker it becomes.

The *Rice Seedling Sutra* describes what happens as we are dying in terms of physical pain, mental anguish and distress, sorrow, and lamentation. Aging and death together form the twelfth link and their negative side is emphasized. If we have been born as a result of contaminated actions underlain by disturbing emotions rooted in ignorance, are we certain to die in the way the sutra describes? The best kind of practitioner dies happily like a well-loved child returning home to the house of its parents. Other practitioners can at least die without fear or regret. They do not experience the anguish and distress described in the sutra because their minds are calm and clear, their death is gentle and they are not tormented by attachment nor by guilt and regret.

It is difficult quickly to stop birth as a result of our actions and disturbing emotions, but since we have a sound body and mind at present, at least we have an opportunity to avoid dying in a state of mental turmoil. As human beings we can think about all this and draw conclusions from it. We can distinguish between what is constructive and what is harmful, and we have the ability to change the quality of our physical, verbal, and mental activities by strengthening our positive attitudes, emotions, and states of mind. If we work at this, we are gradually purifying ourselves and there will be nothing to fear. If we die peacefully in a positive state of mind, it will, of course, be wonderful for us and will move and inspire those close to us.

The stopping of these twelve steps, called the purified side of the process, is also contemplated in forward and reverse sequence. Beginning with the reverse sequence, we think about how aging and the painful process of dying can be stopped. To do this we must stop involuntary birth, which is the result of our contaminated actions. To prevent these actions we must insure that ignorance does not dictate how we act, and ultimately we must uproot that ignorance completely. Similarly, in the forward sequence, we think about how if ignorance is stopped, contaminated actions stop. This prevents birth resulting from such actions, which, in turn, stops aging and death. Through contemplating the process in this forward sequence we come to understand the third noble truth, cessation of suffering, and a wish arises to attain a state in which there is no more birth as a result of contaminated actions and disturbing emotions. Once we have this wish, it becomes clear that the only way of accomplishing it is by practicing true paths of insight, the fourth noble truth. Specifically we need to understand how the self actually exists, which is done by recognizing that what the misconception clings to lacks existence.

Contemplation of this twelve-part process thus enables us to understand that true suffering and true sources of suffering are what we need to get rid of and that the cessation of suffering by means of true paths of insight is what we must accomplish. The reverse sequence associated with the afflicted side, beginning with aging and death, helps us to understand true suffering, while through the reverse sequence associated with the purified side we understand true cessation of suffering. Through contemplation of the afflicted side in forward sequence from ignorance to action and so forth we recognize the need to rid ourselves of the true sources of suffering. Meditation on the purified side in forward sequence, namely how stopping ignorance stops action and therefore stops birth, reveals to us the need to gain true paths of insight.

In his shortest exposition of the stages of the path the great Tibetan master Je Tsongkhapa wrote:[24]

A real aspiration for freedom will not arise
Without effort to reflect on the faults of true suffering.
Unless you consider its source, the stages of
    involvement
In cyclic existence, you won't know how to sever its
    root.
So cultivate aversion to it and a wish for freedom
And cherish the knowledge of what binds you to this
    cycle.

We need to develop an aversion to cyclic existence and the suffering it entails, while understanding correctly what binds us to it. Meditation on the twelve links will help us to do this. It is the highway and if we follow it we can't go wrong. One of the Kadamapa masters, Geshe Puchungwa,[25] pointed out that all the practices and insights of the three levels of intention and capacity[26] are contained within this method of meditation on the twelve-part process of dependent arising.

There are two kinds of rebirth we may take—a good one or a bad one. Aging and dying in a bad state are the result of being born in such a state, which occurs because of harmful actions we have performed. Such actions come from our own ignorance and confusion. Considered in the forward sequence: a moment of ignorance gives rise to a negative action, leading to birth in a bad state, which is then followed by aging and death, so it is vital not to create the causes which could lead to such a rebirth. When we meditate sufficiently on the process that takes us into bad states of rebirth, we will probably feel afraid and want to avoid such an outcome.

The practices of the initial level of capacity in this context consist of taking heartfelt refuge in the Three Jewels, refraining from negative actions, particularly the ten harmful ones,[27] and doing what we can to perform positive actions. This makes us the best kind of initial-level practitioner, closes the door to bad states of rebirth, and insures a good one. Only in this way do we fulfill the most basic criterion of a genuine practitioner of the Buddha's teachings. We can, of course, create virtue without being a true practitioner, which requires that our orientation is at least towards the well-being of future lives.

We also think about aging and death in a good rebirth— one as a human or celestial being—contemplating the sequence of the twelve links in reverse and forward order. Even good rebirths are fraught with suffering. Gaining the strong wish to free ourselves entirely from any kind of rebirth in cyclic existence, even a good one, and doing what is needed for such liberation constitute the practices of the intermediate level of capacity.

In this way we take stock of our own suffering and develop a wish for freedom. Understanding that others' suffering and their wish to be free from it are like our own leads to a deep empathy with them and to the practices of the greatest level of capacity. Without fully understanding our own suffering and without a wish for personal freedom from it, we cannot develop true compassion for others. As we focus on others and contemplate how they are imprisoned in cyclic existence, taking rebirth over and over again and experienc-

ing limitless forms of suffering, love and compassion for
them and the spirit of enlightenment will arise. Our concern
will give us the impetus to work for them in many different
ways which are included in the six perfections.

This is a road map for our own development and it will
also eventually enable us to explain clearly to others the
way the different practices interconnect. We cannot hope to
transform ourselves by constructing fantasies. Transformation must be rooted in reality and based on seeing things as
they actually are.

Is thinking about how others keep taking rebirth in the
different realms of cyclic existence and incessantly experience suffering enough to produce strong love and compassion? Something more is needed: until we see them as very
close, as near, dear, and lovable, their suffering will not
move us or arouse these feelings. This is not difficult to understand because the closer we feel to a person or animal,
the more their suffering has the power to touch us and make
us want to help. When we see those we dislike suffer, we
feel no wish to help them. In fact their suffering may give
us satisfaction. This is because we do not find them lovable
and feel no closeness. Nor do we feel any urgency to help
all those towards whom we are indifferent. The compassion
and love we seek to develop are impartial. They extend to all
living beings and have the power to induce a special wish
to take personal responsibility for their happiness and relief
from suffering. Development of such love and compassion
requires a lot of training.

The Buddha's teaching provides us with methods that
can help us to feel warmth and friendliness towards all living beings. That would bring us great happiness in turn.
As long as we regard others with hostility, see them as our
enemies and feel the need to defend ourselves, we will be
lonely and unhappy even when we are surrounded by peo-

ple. The way we look at things really does determine what we experience.

Others are indeed our friends because they constantly support us even if we don't recognize it. Love and compassion will arise when we train ourselves to see them truly as friends. It is an ideal which we cannot expect to achieve in a short time. At present we have fleeting feelings of warmth and compassion, but they will only become strong and sustained as a result of consciously arousing them again and again.

To begin with we at least need the wish to feel compassionate and loving. If we keep working at it, eventually change begins to occur. It's like building a house. First we need a plan. Then we begin building bit by bit from the foundation upwards. Creating this inner transformation takes a lot of work. We have many different projects. Is to become more loving and compassionate one of them? If not, we will never accomplish it. Even though the Buddha spoke of these things more than two thousand years ago, they are still completely relevant today.

6 THE TWELVE LINKS

In what follows we will examine some different ways of presenting the twelve links but will focus in particular on how they are viewed in the philosophical system based upon the great Indian master Nagarjuna's *Treatise on the Middle Way*. This important work deals almost exclusively with the fundamental nature of reality—namely that all existent phenomena lack any kind of reified, intrinsic, and objective existence. Having demonstrated this, in the twenty-sixth chapter of *The Treatise* Nagarjuna examines the dependently existent nature of the twelve-part process that keeps us bound within cyclic existence and demonstrates how, by stopping the fundamental ignorance which underlies it, we can halt the process step by step.

According to some Buddhist schools of thought all twelve links can occur at the same time in relation to a single action, such as killing an animal out of a desire to eat its meat. At the time of killing, different kinds of confusion—regarding how things exist and regarding the connection between actions and their effects—are present and constitute the first link, ignorance. From this standpoint the intention to kill creates the formative action, the second link. Ignorance and intention are mental factors accompanying primary consciousness which apprehends its object, the third link.

Name and form, the fourth link, are taken to refer to the person's five aggregates at the time of performing the action, while the fifth link, the six sources, refers specifically to that person's faculties, present within the five aggregates. The coming together of these faculties with an object is referred to as contact, the sixth link. This contact between faculty and object produces the experience of pleasure, pain, or what is neutral, which is referred to as feeling, the seventh link.

Attachment, the eighth link, is accompanied by a lack of shame and lack of embarrassment. In general the attachment can either be directed towards pleasure, or it can take the form of a desire to avoid or be rid of pain. Lack of shame is an absence of the self-respect that would prevent us from performing a negative action. Lack of embarrassment means we do not have the decency to take the opinion of others into account, which would normally inhibit us from doing wrong. Lack of shame and embarrassment are the root of all nonvirtue, whereas their opposites serve as the basis for everything good. We live in strange times when people think we need to rid ourselves of these qualities, but to be without them is like running around stark naked.

The ninth link, grasping, is a reaching out for the object of attachment. Readiness for the physical action of killing constitutes the tenth link, existence. The arising of these eleven links and the inception of the action is its birth or production, the eleventh link. The development and disintegration of that action are the twelfth link. The eleventh and twelfth links are sequential, while all the others occur simultaneously.

Production, duration, and disintegration are seen as a sequence and cover the time span of a process. These twelve links take place within that short time span, which is termed an instant.[28] This presentation of the twelve links by certain proponents of the Vaibhashika system of tenets gives us much to think about since every action involves many different factors. There is also a presentation of the process in terms of three lives, referred to as the twelve links at different junctures.[29]

The presentation of the twelve links which we will consider here is substantially different. The order in which they are enumerated may seem perplexing at first but, in fact, it covers first the projecting causes and the projected effects, followed by the accomplishing causes and the accomplished effects.[30]

Ignorance, formative action and consciousness, the latter referring to the imprint implanted on consciousness by the action, are the causes which project another rebirth. The projected effects consist of name and form, the six sources, contact, and feeling. How do ignorance and action project another rebirth? By implanting an imprint on consciousness. To use a farming analogy: ignorance is the farmer and the formative action is the seed. Consciousness is the field in which the seed is sown. When craving and grasping activate this seed or imprint, the next four links, which are the effects, are projected.

There are three accomplishing factors: craving, grasping, and existence. What they accomplish are birth as well as aging and death. They are called accomplishing factors because when craving and grasping activate the imprint, all the different factors required to create a new rebirth become ready for the accomplishment of the result.

First we need to acquaint ourselves with these twelve links and understand this way of presenting them.

In his *Supplement to the Middle Way* the Indian master Chandrakirti says:[31]

If when free and in conducive conditions,
We do not act to restrain ourselves,

We will fall into an abyss and be controlled by others.
How can we later rise up again?

We enjoy great liberty at present because we are free
from all kinds of adverse circumstances and are supported
by many conducive conditions. The first thing we need to do
is to protect ourselves from bad future rebirths by observing
a sound code of ethical discipline, beginning with restraint
from the ten harmful activities. Once we are in a bad state
of existence, it is difficult not to keep taking bad rebirths.
The power of our previous actions and the power of Buddhas
to help us are equal, and even an enlightened being cannot
override the force of our own karma. We must understand
well and without error what needs to be done and what we
must avoid. With our human intelligence we can distinguish
between constructive and detrimental actions, but our present confusion and ignorance prevent us from doing this. Our
spiritual practice should be an effective counteraction to this
confusion and to the clinging attachment, hostility, and all
the other disturbing emotions which come from that confusion. If we can decrease these emotions, we will feel so
much happier.

7 IGNORANCE

The Indian master Atisha used the metaphor of a pig and its activities to illustrate the chaos which confusion causes.[32]

> The pig of ignorance, because of confusion,
> Roots around and digs up the nice clean grass.
> It isn't attracted to places like pure lands
> But takes delight where there is dirt.
> It smacks its lips in the filthy mire.
> And even though its owner will surely kill it,
> The pig of ignorance is deceived by him.
> Without any effort to escape, it enjoys
> The bait of barley beer lees and turnips.

Imagine a lovely well-kept lawn. A pig arrives and makes itself at home. It begins to root around with its snout. In no time it has ruined the lawn completely and destroyed whatever was growing there.

Atisha says that our ethical discipline is like the lawn, and the pig like our confusion regarding the connection between actions and their effects. The pig rooting around with its snout resembles the way we destroy our ethical discipline through careless, confused negative actions. This makes it impossible for good qualities to develop because they can only

grow in the fertile earth of good ethics, which at the most fundamental level means restraint from the ten harmful activities.

Atisha points out that pigs don't like clean places. Similarly, people under the influence of ignorance and confusion dislike monasteries and the kind of quiet and secluded places that
are conducive to spiritual practice. Pigs make for dirty places,
and people governed by confusion head straight for town because they prefer the distraction of worldly activities. Strictly
speaking, these distractions include even business, farming,
and other things people normally do to earn a living.

The pig's owner fattens up the pig so that it will be ready
for slaughter. But the pig is unsuspecting and lolls around,
enjoying the slops it is given with no thought of escaping.
The pig is content with its circumstances and quite unaware
that the very person who is feeding it will one day butcher it.
A benefactor gives his support to a monk, for example, and
that support is valuable because without the necessities of
life the monk cannot devote himself to practice. But gradually the benefactor and the monk become more intimate. They
begin to consult on various matters.

One day they discuss how the monk can gather all the resources needed to support the practice he hopes to do in the
future. The benefactor makes useful suggestions, and before
long the monk becomes involved in the enterprise of making
a livelihood. Never mind about remaining ordained, he goes
to the opposite extreme. He plunges more fully into secular
life than a lay person and has no scruples about doing all
kinds of negative things. This is like the slaughter because it
kills all chances of happiness and excellence. Such a sorry
state of affairs is the result of ignorance.

To give another simile, ignorance is like the king, and
clinging attachment and hostility are his ministers. To rid ourselves of the king's minions we must get rid of the king. And
so it is of greatest importance to identify ignorance properly.

The twenty-sixth chapter of the great Nagarjuna's *Treatise on the Middle Way*, called *Examining the Twelve Links of Existence*, is based on the Buddha's words in the *Rice Seedling Sutra* and other sutras, but the way in which Nagarjuna has presented the subject-matter is extremely terse and concise. If we understand these verses well, they provide us with an excellent guide to meditation on how we remain trapped in cyclic existence and how we can free ourselves. In this commentary we will attempt to unpack each verse and consider some of its ramifications in detail.

Nagarjuna begins the twenty-sixth chapter with the following words:

1
Obscured by ignorance, existence recurs
From performing any of the three kinds
Of formative actions through which
One goes on to another rebirth.

What is meant by ignorance in this context? There are different views about this; however, ignorance here does not mean merely a failure to understand reality nor does it mean not understanding something other than reality. Rather, it is the opposite of the understanding that the person and other phenomena lack intrinsic existence. Those who are affected by this ignorance create actions which precipitate them into further worldly existence.

Formative actions are nonvirtuous, virtuous, or unfluctuating actions.[33] Nagarjuna's words can also be taken to refer to physical, verbal, and mental activities. They are called formative because they form the body and mind of the next rebirth. Someone obscured by ignorance does not necessarily perform a particular action with any thought of future rebirth, but the action begins the formative process whether this was intended or not. The person is propelled into the next rebirth through the force of such actions.

All systems of Buddhist philosophical tenets hold that ignorance is incompatible with knowledge and prevents correct understanding. The word for ignorance in Tibetan is *ma rig pa. Ma* is a negative particle. *Rig pa* means knowing or understanding. In his *Compendium of Knowledge* Asanga says that the ignorance which is incompatible with correct understanding is a confusion with regard to the fundamental nature of the object and not a misunderstanding of it. According to him ignorance prevents a person from gaining an understanding of reality through hearing, thinking, and meditating. It is an obstacle to clear perception of reality and functions like darkness, which hides the objects in a room even from someone with good sight.

Through the influence of this confusion and lack of clarity, an object which has no existence in and of itself is seen to exist in this way. For Asanga this distorting perception is a false view of the transitory collection.[34] He distinguishes between ignorance and this, which to him is an aspect of apprehension, albeit improper apprehension, because the mind actually engages with and examines its object, whereas ignorance does not have the ability to apprehend its object.

Asanga describes it as a process consisting of two steps: confusion and lack of clarity lead to misperception. From this come clinging attachment and hostility, which in turn lead to the kinds of actions that keep us in cyclic existence.

The following example illustrates the way Asanga describes the process. When you see a coiled mottled rope in front of you on a path at dusk, the lack of light prevents you from seeing clearly. This leads to a misapprehension of what is there as a snake and you feel frightened.

If someone is not your friend, it doesn't necessarily mean he is your foe, but the opposite of a friend is a foe, just as the opposite of truth is falsehood and the opposite of being loving is to be unloving. Not understanding something is not the opposite of understanding it correctly. For the great Indian masters Dharmakirti,[35] Bhavaviveka[36] (who promulgated what came to be known as the Svantantrika-Madhyamika view), and Chandrakirti (who put forward the Prasangika-Madhyamika view), ignorance is more than a lack of understanding. They assert that it is diametrically opposed to the understanding of reality gained through hearing, thinking, and meditating, and that it is incompatible with the exalted knowledge that understands reality correctly.[37] According to them ignorance is a distorted perception of the object and a deluded form of understanding.[38]

We all experience times when our mind seems to be shrouded in darkness and we cannot think clearly. This is a sign that confusion is at work, but there are more subtle levels of confusion that we do not notice. Do our minds actually engage with reality? At present they do not because ignorance prevents us from perceiving the fundamental condition of things and conceals reality from us.

In his *Praise for Dependent Arising*[39] Je Tsongkhapa writes:

Through what you realized and proclaimed
The foremost knower and guide. Subduer,
I bow to you who saw and taught
Dependent relativity.

Whatever troubles of this world
Their root is ignorance. You taught
The insight that reverses it,
Dependent relativity.

He extols the Buddha Shakyamuni as an authentic teacher for having understood fully and correctly how we remain implicated in cyclic existence and how we can extricate ourselves; for practicing what he had understood, attaining enlightenment, and communicating his understanding to others. If we practice what the Buddha taught, we will not only be able to transcend repeated involuntary birth, sickness, aging, and death but also go beyond the limitations associated with a state of personal peace. At the root of all our problems is the misconception that the self and other phenomena are truly existent. By understanding that nothing exists in this way and by familiarizing ourselves with it, we will gradually be able to free ourselves from all these troubles.

In the *Praise for Dependent Arising* Je Tsongkhapa also writes:

Who turn away from what you taught
May long perform austerities,
Yet they, so fixed their view of self,
But summon faults repeatedly.

If we follow those who assert that both the physical world and the living beings in it were created by some kind of permanent self or eternal creator, perform austere practices, and perhaps even succeed in accomplishing states of profound concentration, we may be born in the highest rebirth within cyclic existence, the Peak of Existence, and remain in deep absorption for many aeons. But one day the momentum of our meditative stabilization will come to an end and we will be forced once more to take rebirth in the desire realm, where we must experience ordinary birth, sickness, aging, death, and the many other troubles that afflict us. We will simply have beckoned to all these problems, because despite our intensive practice our misconception of the self remained intact and firmly in place. As long as it persists, everything that springs from it will arise automatically.

For these reasons the wise learn to distinguish between the Buddha and his teaching and other teachers and their teachings. Understanding the differences well, we should avoid those systems of thought and practice that do not enable us to address the root of our problems. When we fully understand the profundity of the Buddha's teaching on the dependently arising nature of everything that exists, it will not fail to move us. We will get goose pimples, the tears will well up in our eyes, and we will quite naturally want to place our palms together in a gesture of respect and homage. Expressing this awe in the *Praise for Dependent Arising,* Je Tsongkhapa writes:

> As teacher, refuge, orator
> Or guardian—how astonishing!
> I bow to you who taught so well
> Dependent relativity.

We must identify clearly what kind of ignorance acts as a cause for further cyclic existence and what kind does not. We must also examine how other disturbing emotions develop from ignorance, which serves as their basis, and how this influences our physical and verbal activities and affects our experience of happiness and suffering. Once we are fully convinced that everything unwanted happens because of ignorance, we will examine whether or not it is possible to get rid of this ignorance, and if so, how.

The true reason why the Buddha's teachings are passed on and why it is worth considering this matter of the twelve links is in order to get rid of suffering. When we listen to the teachings, we should not be intent on hearing something new and interesting. Our attention should be firmly directed inwards and we should take the teachings very personally, constantly relating them to ourselves and to the search to discover the real cause of our difficulties.

There are many forms of negative physical and verbal behavior that most societies legislate against because they consider them detrimental. They come from our turbulent emotions, but usually only people involved in spiritual practice recognize the need to curtail the emotions that motivate undesirable actions. If we want to get rid of them, we must learn to recognize them and understand how they function and how they affect us. We must know their immediate and long-term effects, how we can deal with them quickly when emergency measures need to be taken, and how we can rid ourselves of them completely by stopping the ignorance from which they stem.

Just as non-attachment counters attachment and benevolence counters hostility, only the correct understanding of reality can counter ignorance, its antithesis. These three basic disturbing states of mind—attachment, hostility, and confusion—spawn all other disturbing emotions and negativity. Their opposites engender all virtue and everything positive. To rid ourselves of attachment we must develop a sincere wish for freedom from cyclic existence, and to overcome anger we must become more loving. To rid ourselves of ignorance we have to understand the dependently arising nature of things and their emptiness of intrinsic existence.

Mental activity is classified as primary mental activity, which consists of the different kinds of consciousness, and secondary mental activities.[40] Ignorance, which is the opposite of a correct understanding of things, is not one of the six kinds of consciousness but a secondary mental activity.

Ignorance can be of two types: afflicted ignorance, which is a disturbing attitude, and non-afflicted ignorance. The former may be either a misconception of the self or that which is not a misconception of the self. There is afflicted ignorance which is a disturbing attitude but not a misconception of the self. Examples of this are confusion with regard to the connection between actions and their effects; ignorance that regards what is impermanent as permanent or what is painful as pleasurable; ignorance with respect to the four noble truths; and ignorance accompanying clinging attachment, desire, anger, doubt, or any other disturbing emotion. All disturbing emotions are accompanied by ignorance which, as it were, eggs them on and lends them support. When we become foe destroyers[41] we have rid ourselves of these diverse forms of ignorance.

However, foe destroyers still have non-afflicted ignorance. For instance, although they have understanding of the connection between actions and their effects, they do not perceive the most subtle aspects of karma, such as which specific actions have produced a particular result. Only a fully enlightened one has complete knowledge of this. Foe destroyers know that enlightened beings possess extraordinary qualities, without fully understanding what those qualities are. Believing that there is no connection between actions and their effects, such as is postulated in the Buddha's teachings, or believing that enlightened beings do not possess the qualities ascribed to them constitutes a wrong view. In the case of foe destroyers, however, there is no lack of conviction but a lack of full understanding.

We have spoken about ignorance in general and have also considered the particular kind of ignorance which forms the first of the twelve links. We have a very strong feeling of an "I" and we cling to this. As long as we have not understood that this self, which appears so vividly, is something nonexistent, the ignorance which is the first of the twelve links—the misconception of our own self—will continue to arise and cause us to act.

The misconception of our own self is referred to as the false view of the transitory collection as a real "I" and "mine." It springs from a misconception of the aggregates, which constitute body and mind. This is referred to as the misconception of a self of phenomena. These two underlie our cyclic existence and are the source of our suffering.

There are forms of ignorance that act as the root of cyclic existence which do not constitute the first link of this twelve-part process. There is also ignorance which is the first link but does not act as a root of cyclic existence and there are forms of ignorance that are both, and others which are neither.

An example of ignorance that acts as a root of cyclic existence but which is not the first link of this twelve-part process is the innate misconception of the aggregates that constitute body and mind as truly existent. An example of the second kind of ignorance mentioned is an intellectually formed conception of a truly existent self, namely one acquired through philosophical speculation or through misleading instruction.

The first of the twelve links, which also acts as a root of cyclic existence, is a misconception of the self that is present in all living beings and must therefore be the instinctive or innate kind. Ignorance accompanying desire, anger, and so forth is neither the first link nor does it act as the root of cyclic existence.

8 ACTION AND REBIRTH

Ignorance gives impetus to an action by providing the motivating force. Ignorance precedes the second link, formative action, functioning in a causal capacity, and it is also present with the action.[42] This ignorance can be of two kinds: ignorance regarding the fundamental nature of things and ignorance regarding the connection between actions and their effects. Both may accompany formative action, but when a virtuous action is performed, the second type of ignorance regarding the connection between actions and their effects is absent. The contemporaneous motivating ignorance pushes the action through to its conclusion. If ignorance about the connection between actions and their effects is present, virtuous action will not occur.

A negative action, such as killing, may be motivated by desire, anger, or confusion. We may slaughter an animal because of our desire to eat meat. If someone has harmed us, we may kill that person out of anger and the wish to take revenge. We may wrongly believe that blood sacrifice will bring us good fortune. These are examples of the motivating forces that can cause us to act. Lack of mercy and aggression are active when we kill for any of these reasons. Although ignorance is present, this ignorance is not the kind that forms the first of the twelve links—that ignorance is always the instinctive misconception of our own self.[43]

How do the disturbing emotions arise from the misconception of the self? First there is a very vivid sense of self. When the innate sense of this larger-than-life "I" is present, a particularly sharp distinction is made between oneself and others. There is, of course, an "I" and there are "others," but when the misconception is operating, these two are viewed in a special way that gives rise both to strong attachment to the self together with everything we consider to be on our side, and to aversion towards anything we see as other and hostile. From that distinction and from the strong sense of "me" and "mine" comes a clinging to my happiness and the happiness of those associated with me and fear and repugnance to anything that threatens it.

Then we act—physically, verbally, or mentally—to insure our happiness, to prevent others from interfering with it, and to protect ourselves from what we perceive as harm. Meritorious, demeritorious, or unfluctuating actions that are the result of ignorance keep us within cyclic existence.

We have taken rebirth over and over again throughout time without beginning. Helplessly we keep experiencing all the suffering associated with cyclic existence. To break out of this process we must stop the formative actions that yield their results enabled by craving and grasping. This can only be done by ridding ourselves of attachment and hostility and the underlying ignorance.

In this context particular emphasis is laid on getting rid of the attachment or craving. Freeing ourselves from this is no easy matter because our notion of the self is deeply entrenched and habitual. It will be of no help to look outwards. We must look for the root of cyclic existence within ourselves, examine how the misconception arises, how it serves as a foundation for the other disturbing attitudes and emotions, and how it can be uprooted.

All ordinary living beings have this misconception and act under its influence. Exalted beings have direct perception of reality as it actually is, and though they may still have confusion, it no longer influences their actions, so they do not act in ways that perpetuate their existence in the round of rebirth.

We create many positive and negative actions. Are all the actions we perform the kind that will give rise to another rebirth with a suffering body and mind? Is there ever a time when we are not creating actions that will give rise to further cyclic existence? We act even in our dreams. Will these actions, too, perpetuate cyclic existence?

Through appreciating the marvelous qualities of enlightenment, we may aspire to become enlightened ourselves and create meritorious actions for that purpose. Or having heard about the many disadvantages of cyclic existence and thought about them, we may perform virtuous actions with a strong antipathy to our present condition and with a wish to free ourselves. We may receive teachings on emptiness and, with our own limited understanding, contemplate it and try to recall the nature of reality when we act.

Will these positive actions produce a good rebirth? If so, are all of these actions simply producing further cyclic existence, albeit in one of the better states? Is the attainment of high status, namely a good rebirth, necessarily the result of formative actions? Aren't the actions we have just mentioned, such as those motivated by the wish for freedom from cyclic existence, for liberation and enlightenment, the antidote to cyclic existence?

These are meritorious actions based on turning away from cyclic existence. If we think everything we do at present is simply going to give rise to further cyclic existence, it is very discouraging. We should understand that it is possible for us at this moment to perform actions that will not do this, which is why so much emphasis is laid on motivation. Not all thought is counterproductive. The result of our actions depends upon our intention, and thoughts that are directed towards the attainment of liberation, for instance, are constructive thoughts. If they are strong enough, the actions which arise from them will act as causes for freedom from cyclic existence.

In the chapter on perseverance in his *Way of the Bodhisattva* Shantideva says:[44]

> Take advantage of this human boat;
> Free yourself from sorrow's mighty stream!
> This vessel will be later hard to find.
> The time that you have now, you fool, is not for sleep!

Using this good body and mind in the right way, we can free ourselves from suffering. No other rebirth offers us such an opportunity. As an animal we have no chance of liberation or enlightenment. To accomplish this task we will need at least several more rebirths, for even though it is possible to do it in one lifetime, if we consider our own intelligence and the amount of effort we are prepared to make, it will certainly take time. So we must try in every way to insure that we take the kind of rebirths in the future that can provide us with the very best conditions for practice.

Unless we enjoy the favorable circumstances that make good consistent practice possible, we will not see any significant results, no matter how much effort we make to gain insights. A number of factors make a human rebirth special and privileged. The eight freedoms and ten riches distinguish a precious human life from an ordinary one.[45] There are also eight assets which result from positive past actions and seven distinguishing attributes. Ideally we possess a working basis endowed with the "four wheels" that can speed us towards enlightenment in the Great Vehicle.

Possession of the eight freedoms and ten riches means that we are free from all kinds of hindrances that prevent practice and enjoy conducive circumstances that support it. The eight assets that come from past virtue are a long life span, an attractive appearance, birth into a good family, authority and wealth, trustworthy speech, a strong body and mind, and being male. If one possesses these eight, one also probably has the seven features that distinguish a high state of rebirth. The "four wheels" are to live in a conducive place; to have a relationship with an excellent or holy being; to admire and take an interest in excellent activities, such as the pursuit of liberation and enlightenment, with a strong aspiration to practice accordingly; and to have created a good store of positive energy.[46]

We should examine whether we enjoy all these advantages and make sure that we will have them in the future as well. A good body and mind are essential, but we also need a long life, otherwise there will not be enough time to accomplish anything in our practices. We need time now and sufficient time in the future. Just praying for this is not enough. We have to create the causes that give rise to a long life.

Just as most of us like to be attractive to others and to have a good appearance now, we will also want that in the future. This is not frivolous because if we look nice, we can more easily create relationships with others and through that find many opportunities to help them. It will also make it easier to get whatever material support we need to sustain our practice.

Patience gives rise to an attractive appearance. This is self-evident because people who are even-tempered, calm, and patient attract others, even though they may not be beautiful in a conventional sense. Those who are truly patient are also loving, which makes them very appealing. When we get upset and angry, we are not at all attractive to others. If we wish to have certain qualities, we have to make effort to develop them, since things do not just happen causelessly.

One of the assets mentioned in this context is that we will be born with status. This is desirable because the ability to command respect and esteem will decrease the obstacles we face when working for others. Such status is the result of showing respect to those who possess admirable qualities and have done good. We must, therefore, avoid denigrating and condescending conduct towards others.

We also need sufficient resources to practice without having to worry about daily necessities. If we have plenty, we can easily attract others through generosity and do many things for their benefit.

Our speech should be honest and convey what needs to be said in a sincere way. Our own actions should accord with the advice we give others. These qualities will serve us well now and in the future, so we should take this precious opportunity to create their causes now. We need the best possible conditions if we are to use our body and mind to free ourselves.

Like us, animals try to avoid the suffering of pain, and practitioners in many spiritual traditions endeavor to overcome preoccupation with ordinary or contaminated pleasure, which is untrustworthy and subject to change. Buddhist practice is unique in providing us with the means to free ourselves from the constraints of having this kind of body and mind, which are the result of contaminated actions and disturbing emotions and constitute the pervasive suffering of conditioning. These compulsive actions and the disturbing emotions are the second noble truth, the true sources of suffering that bind us to cyclic existence and make true suffering, the first noble truth, inevitable. A deeper exploration of the four noble truths brings us to the teaching on the twelve links of dependent arising, which is a cherished treasure among the jewels of the Buddha's teachings and is worth thinking about again and again.

As we have seen, when ignorance regarding the fundamental nature of things and ignorance regarding the connection between actions and their effects are both present, the result is a negative action which leads to a bad rebirth. In other cases, only the former but not the latter kind of ignorance is present. We could be aware that positive actions lead to happiness but mistake the happiness of good rebirths for real happiness without recognizing the suffering entailed. As a result we might perform all kinds of positive actions in order to be reborn as a human or celestial being. These are meritorious actions that are still underlain by the misconception of the self.

Formative action in this context means action motivated by ignorance belonging to the same set of twelve links, since several sets of the twelve links ordinarily are operating simultaneously. This action will project a number of factors that also belong to the same set of twelve links. Action, according to the lower schools of tenets, refers to the mental factor of intention; however, from the Prasangika point of view, physical and verbal actions have physical form. Action can be created through any of the three doors of body, speech, and mind.

Demeritorious action consists of such actions as the seven harmful activities of body and speech, while meritorious action is virtuous action which avoids these seven.[47] Unfluctuating action refers to practices of deep concentration that give rise to rebirth in the upper realms of celestial beings in deep states of absorption. This kind of action can only be created if we have accomplished a calmly abiding mind. Formative action forms the next existence. The action does this even though the person may be totally unaware or unmindful of its consequences.

The moment the action ceases, it leaves an imprint on consciousness. The third link is called consciousness and refers to that moment when the action stops and the seed is implanted. This is consciousness at the time of the cause, or causal consciousness. Consciousness at the moment of conception in the rebirth resulting from this imprint is referred to as resultant consciousness.

Ignorance, formative action, and consciousness are the three projecting causes. The results they project are name and form, the six sources, contact, and feeling. Craving and grasping, like moisture and a fertile growing medium, activate the seed-like imprint so that it begins to grow.

We all have a vast store of imprints from the countless positive and negative actions we have performed. Only mental consciousness, not any of the five kinds of sensory consciousness, acts as the storehouse. Although this consciousness changes moment by moment, it continues in an unbroken continuity, whereas there are periods, such as during sleep, when the different kinds of sensory consciousness stop operating. Whether we take a good or bad rebirth depends on what sort of imprint ripens. Since mental consciousness continues on to that new rebirth, the person imputed to that consciousness does so too.

2

Conditioned by formative action,
Consciousness enters rebirths.
When consciousness has entered,
Name and form come into being.

A variety of causes and conditions produce each moment of consciousness, but here Nagarjuna emphasizes how formative action determines which kind of rebirth the consciousness will enter. How does consciousness continue on? It does so when the death process is complete and the moment of death occurs. This is simultaneous with the beginning of the intermediate state. In the case of a human rebirth, the being of the intermediate state ceases to exist at the moment when consciousness enters the fertilized ovum in the womb of the mother. The end of the intermediate existence and the beginning of the human existence are simultaneous. The final moment of the death process is like deep sleep; the intermediate state is like dreaming and conception like waking.

The fourth link, name and form, describes the moment of conception. "Name" refers to the four aggregates of feeling, discrimination, compositional factors, and consciousness, while "form" refers to the physical embryo. The entity of the being has come into existence, after which development takes place.

Just as barley seed or rice seed yield their own specific crop, the imprints implanted on consciousness through performing actions yield their own particular results in the form of good or bad rebirths. When rebirth in the desire realm or form realm occurs, all five aggregates are present from the very beginning. In the formless realm the four aggregates associated with mental activity are present, but since beings in that realm have no actual physical form, the physical aspect is present only as a potential.

9 EXPERIENCE AND RESPONSE

The next verses of Nagarjuna's text show how the capacity to experience arises and how response to experience takes place while the unborn child is growing.

> 3
> **When name and form have come into being,**
> **The six sources emerge.**
> **In dependence on these six sources**
> **Contact properly arises.**

Gradually the fetus develops and the six sources—from the eye sense faculty to the mental faculty—are formed.[48] The bases for these faculties are there from the outset, but this link is called the six sources because now the sources have developed and can function. The mental faculty and mental consciousness in a subtle form are present from the moment of conception.

At conception the entity of the living being came into existence. The attributes of that living being emerge with the development of the six sources and it now becomes a user of things, namely one who can engage with things. All of this is the maturation of an action performed in the past.

What are the conditions that give rise to contact? In the third verse Nagarjuna underlines the vital role played by the faculties when he writes, "In dependence on these six sources contact properly arises." However, a number of other factors are also important. The first two lines of the fourth verse indicate the various conditions which enable contact to occur.

4
It arises only through the eye,
A form, and that which remembers.
Therefore consciousness arises
In dependence on name and form.

For instance, a moment of visual consciousness arises through the main condition, the eye sense faculty, and through the focal condition, which is a visible form. The words "that which remembers" refer to the immediately preceding condition, which is any immediately preceding moment of awareness.

Nagarjuna says, "Consciousness arises in dependence on name and form." In this context "name" refers to the preceding moment of mental activity and "form" to the visual object and the eye sense faculty. The latter two are both matter and are therefore regarded as form. A moment of visual consciousness occurs through the meeting or coming together of a visible form, the visual sense faculty, which resides in the eye, and a moment of awareness.

In the case of the child in the womb, mental consciousness and the mental faculty are present from the outset, and the moment of preceding mental activity, which occurs before visual perception can arise for the first time, is a moment of attention accompanying mental consciousness.[49]

5
**Contact is a combination of three—
Eye, form, and consciousness—
And from such contact
Feeling always arises.**

Although Nagarjuna's words appear to say that the coming together of the eye, form, and consciousness is contact, contact is actually the consequence of their coming together and is the ability to discern whether objects, such as smells, sounds, or tastes, are pleasant, unpleasant, or neutral. Contact occurs in association with any of the six kinds of consciousness through the presence of the faculty, the focal object, and a moment of awareness.

From contact, which enables distinction between what is agreeable, disagreeable, and neutral, feeling arises. Contact is the experience of the object, while feeling is the experience of maturation.[50] Here maturation or fruition refers to pleasurable, painful, or neutral feelings or sensations that are a maturation or fruition of our past actions.

In relation to pleasant objects, agreeable feelings or sensations arise, while disagreeable feelings or sensations arise in relation to unpleasant objects. Neutral feelings are the response to objects discerned as neither attractive nor unattractive. With the development of the six sources while the fetus is in the womb, the utilizer or experiencer[51] comes into being and when feeling occurs experience is complete.

Craving, grasping, and existence are the accomplishing causes. A seed produces either rice or barley depending on the kind of seed it is, but it needs moisture and a growing medium in order to sprout. While the seed determines the crop, it can only produce that crop if certain other conditions pertain. For the imprint implanted on consciousness to produce name and form, the six sources, contact, feeling, birth, and aging and death, certain factors must come into play. When the seed-like imprint comes into contact with moisture-like craving[52] and grasping, it begins to sprout.

6
Conditioned by feeling there is craving
And the craving is for feeling.
Whenever there is this craving
Grasping of four kinds arises.

In a particular set of the twelve links this craving occurs in a lifetime immediately prior to the one in which the fetus experiences feeling as described above. The feeling on which the craving focuses is associated with the body and mind belonging to a different set of twelve links. The craving and grasping which triggered the imprint that produced this life occurred in a past life. More craving and grasping in this life will activate a dormant imprint and give rise to another rebirth.

The craving directed towards feelings is a desire not to be separated from pleasurable feelings, to be separated from painful feelings, and for neutral feelings not to decline.

The craving related to pleasurable feelings may be to experience past pleasurable feelings again and not to lose what pleasure we enjoy at present. We also constantly reach out for future pleasure. The strong craving to avoid or end painful feelings can lead to a desire for self-destruction. People commit suicide because they cannot bear the suffering they are experiencing. There are many forms of craving associated with the three realms of existence.[53] As our craving to experience pleasure and to be rid of suffering grows stronger, it induces grasping, an intensified form of craving.

Nagarjuna's text says that grasping of four kinds occurs as a result of craving that focuses on feelings: grasping at the objects of the senses, which are what we desire; grasping at philosophical views; grasping at different forms of ethical discipline and modes of conduct as supreme; and grasping at the self.[54]

Grasping at the objects of the senses is strong craving for visible forms, sounds, smells, tastes, or tactile sensations. In this context craving for the sense objects is an appreciation of them, as well as a desire for our experience of them and the enjoyment they induce not to stop. The grasping is a reaching out to experience that joy in the future. Ordinary lay people are primarily involved in this kind of craving and grasping.

The second kind of grasping refers to people's adherence to views through which they hope to find happiness. The false view of the transitory collection is not included in these views.

The third kind of grasping is at misguided forms of discipline and conduct associated with wrong views. This includes attachment to extreme ascetic practices, such as applying fire to different parts of the body, fasting for long periods, physical mutilation, imitating the behavior of pigs or dogs, and all exaggerated forms of austerity. People perform such practices in the hope of purifying wrongdoing and finding happiness.

The final kind of grasping described here is at views of the self, which refers principally to the false view of the transitory collection and pride in oneself. The eighth and ninth links are both disturbing emotions. The grasping emerges from the craving which has preceded it and produces existence, the tenth link. Craving focuses on this life and is attachment to it, while grasping is attachment to and a reaching out for future existence. The craving and grasping activate the imprint that was left on consciousness by formative action and make it ready to produce the next existence.

The tenth link marks complete readiness—and is the cause—for the body and mind of the next existence, so actually the name of the result has been given to the cause. It is like a seed that has come into contact with moisture and a growing medium and that is on the verge of sprouting.

We might think that the activation of an imprint created by a positive action could only occur through constructive thoughts or feelings and not through disturbing emotions such as craving and grasping. Even if at death our state of mind is constructive, an element of craving and grasping will be present. Normally a lot of emphasis is placed on dying in a peaceful frame of mind with feelings of faith or kindness, because out of the many imprints we have this will trigger one that can lead to a good rebirth.[55] It is also said that if we die with attachment or anger, for instance, this will activate a negative imprint and lead to a bad rebirth, so we must do whatever we can to insure neither we nor those we are helping die in a disturbed state.

When we ordinary people are dying, our mind becomes unclear because we do not have control over it. Even if our thoughts are positive, clinging to the self and to the well-being of the self are also active. When there is no clinging to the self, there is no fear. Grasping in the form of anxiety concerning our future well-being could have the beneficial effect of inducing us to make heartfelt prayers to our spiritual teachers or meditational deity. This would then insure a good rebirth.

7
When there is grasping, existence
Of the one who grasps occurs.
When there is no grasping, one is freed
And will not come into existence.

Grasping induces the state of readiness for the next rebirth, which is the tenth link. It is followed by conception and the new life. For those who understand the emptiness of all existent things and have familiarized themselves with it, craving related to feelings does not arise because they perceive the true nature of those feelings. The grasping, since it is intensified craving, cannot arise either, thereby preventing the occurrence of the tenth link.

Gaining a direct or nondual understanding of reality does not instantly liberate us, but those who have a direct perception of reality will not take rebirth again in cyclic existence as a result of contaminated actions underlain by the disturbing emotions. Through continued familiarization with this direct perception of reality, we will eventually gain complete freedom from cyclic existence.

8
Existence, moreover, is the five aggregates.
Through existence birth occurs.
Aging, death, and sorrow,
Lamentation and suffering,

9
Unhappiness and distress
All come from being born.
Thus these exclusively painful
Aggregates come into being.

Existence is the state where the imprint has been fully activated and is ready to yield the aggregates of the next rebirth. It is classed as action and is itself in the nature of the five aggregates: forms, feelings, discriminations, compositional factors, and the different kinds of consciousness.

How are the five aggregates associated with action in this context? Action may be virtuous or nonvirtuous, and can be performed either physically, verbally, or mentally. From the point of view of the Chittamatrins and Svatantrikas, physical and verbal action are not classed as form but as intention, which is a mental factor or function. However, in any discussion of the twelve links from the Prasangika viewpoint, physical and verbal activities are considered to be form. Mental activity includes the aggregates of feeling and discrimination, while other mental functions belong to the aggregate of compositional factors. Accompanying these mental functions are different kinds of consciousness. Thus all five aggregates may be present. When the imprint of the previous virtuous or nonvirtuous action has been triggered through craving and grasping, mental activity related to that imprint and the subtle physical and verbal expressions of that mental activity take place as death approaches. These constitute the link of existence and, as it were, attract and act as a bridge to the aggregates of the subsequent life.

When the first three links—ignorance, formative action, and consciousness—occur, name and form, the six sources, contact, and feeling, which are their projected result, do not yet exist. Once the seed has been implanted in consciousness, it will produce these four effects when it meets with the right conditions.

10 BIRTH, AGING, AND DEATH

For name and form, the six sources, contact, feeling, birth, and aging and death to occur, the six causal factors—ignorance, formative action, consciousness, craving, grasping, and existence—must have taken place. When the process is spread over two lives, the first three of the twelve links—ignorance, formative action, and consciousness—and the eighth and ninth—craving and grasping—occur in one life and all the others in the next life. Where the process extends over more than two lives, the first three steps take place in one life, the eighth and ninth steps in another, and the others in the following life.

The three projecting causes and their four projected results are presented first. They are followed by the accomplishing causes—craving, grasping, and existence—and by birth and aging and death, which are their results.

Sometimes birth, the eleventh link, is interpreted in the conventional way to mean the emergence of the baby from the womb. Usually, however, the consciousness of the living being at the moment of conception in the womb is defined as birth and is simultaneous with the fourth link, name and form. Consciousness at this point is referred to as resultant consciousness, whereas it is termed causal consciousness at the moment when the imprint of the action was implanted.

We have used the example of conception in the womb as a human or mammal. The greatest number of beings take a miraculous birth, although we find this difficult to believe because we do not see it. Celestial beings and those in the hell realms are born in this way. Beings are also born from eggs and through heat but the fundamental process is the same.

These days there are many good books about the development of the fetus in the womb and the description in the Buddhist texts of what occurs compares quite well with what we can see from photographic evidence. People have different ideas about what the unborn child experiences in the womb. Some say it is a pleasurable state, but from a Buddhist point of view it is considered a traumatic experience first to be confined in an increasingly uncomfortable space and then to be forced out through the birth canal. When we are born, we are incapable of speaking about it and by the time we can express ourselves, we no longer remember what we experienced in the womb.

Although it may become possible to produce human beings who have not developed in the womb, all of us humans who are in this world at present have spent some time in the womb and have gone through the experience of being born. Better to grow in the womb of a mother who is capable of loving feelings for the unborn child than to grow in a glass dish! While they were pregnant, most of our mothers took great care that no harm should come to us.

Those who claim that the fetus experiences well-being in the womb are relying on appearances and cannot recall the experience themselves. Ordinary people cannot, of course, remember it as an unpleasant experience either, but great masters with abilities far beyond our own have alluded to the unpleasantness of the fetus's condition. Perhaps the situation of the fetus is a little like that of a prisoner who prefers the security of the jail to the insecurity of the world outside. This does not mean that a jail is a pleasant place.

Aging and death are combined as one link. Aging starts the moment after conception, as the body begins to develop. It always occurs before death even in the case of an unborn child that dies in the womb. All of us, whether young or old, are experiencing the twelfth link now and what is left is death. But conventionally, of course, we speak of aging when our hair turns grey and then white, when our teeth fall out and our faculties begin to deteriorate. Aging is the ripening of the aggregates and death is the process of giving up the aggregates. Aging, death and sorrow, lamentation and suffering are all the result of being born.

Nagarjuna speaks of sorrow, lamentation, suffering, unhappiness, and distress. These are not included within the twelve links because it is possible to die without experiencing them if we perform many positive actions and practice sincerely during our lives. Why then does Nagarjuna mention these emotions and their expression? Since we have been born in cyclic existence, there is a strong possibility that we will die like this. By drawing our attention to it, Nagarjuna reminds us of the disadvantages of our present condition.

We have been born and are definitely going to die, but we still have the opportunity to insure that we will not die in distress. We cannot afford to wait until we are actually dying. Now is the time to prepare and familiarize ourselves with what will prevent such a death. If we do this properly, it is possible to die with joy at leaving behind a decrepit and troublesome body to take a good rebirth full of potential. But if at death we are confused and full of craving and grasping, suffering is inevitable.

In general, existence and cyclic existence have the same meaning. Sometimes four types of existence are presented. The first is intermediate existence. This refers to the aggregates during the period between existence at death and existence at rebirth, and it is a relatively subtle state. The second is existence at birth, referring to the aggregates at conception, which can be equated with the eleventh link, birth.

Preparatory existence extends from the moment after conception until the moment of death, which indicates that our life is a preparation for death. Some commentators have misinterpreted the term *preparatory existence* and have taken it to refer to the intermediate state that follows death. People often mistakenly think that the being in the intermediate state looks like the deceased person. When we die and become a being in the intermediate state, we do not look like the person who died but like the being we will become in our next rebirth. Finally there is existence at death, which is the moment of death itself.[56]

The eleventh link may be taken to refer just to the moment of conception, to the period from conception until conventional birth has taken place, or to the period extending from conception until death. In any case aging begins immediately after we have been conceived. Aging is the moment-by-moment change that occurs while the continuum of aggregates of a similar type persists. Giving up the aggregates of a similar type marks death.

As we die, confusion and clinging to the self are present, which Nagarjuna refers to as sorrow. The verbal expression of this grief and sorrow is lamentation. As the power of the physical senses diminishes, there is suffering. The mental anguish that accompanies this is termed unhappiness. As a result of the physical and mental experiences that occur all kinds of delusions arise and we feel acute distress. Where does all of this come from? From being born. Through the force of the various causes and conditions described in the twelve-part process this aggregation of suffering comes into being.

The text says, "Thus these exclusively painful aggregates come into being." The word *exclusively* is loaded with meaning. It implies that these painful aggregates are totally unrelated to happiness, are not in any way connected with a real "I" or "mine," and that they are merely attributed by naming. They have come into existence through a variety of causes and conditions—in this case the projecting causes and the accomplishing causes as well as many other factors—therefore they have no intrinsic existence in and of themselves and are merely an aggregation of suffering, a collection of suffering, an accumulation of suffering. They exist nominally as a mere attribution dependent on a panoply of causes and conditions.

11 ADVICE ABOUT ACTIONS

When the body and mind of this life separate, the person of
this life ceases but the person is not like a candle that has
gone out, for though the coarse body and mind have ceased
to function, a subtle form of body and mind, to which the
person is attributed, continues to another life.

In the case of a seed we cannot pinpoint a beginning: it
came from a particular plant, which came from a seed that
came from a plant and so on. But we can observe the end of
that cycle when, for instance, the seed is completely burned.
Similarly, we cannot pinpoint a beginning to our rebirths,
but when we have understood reality directly the end of our
cyclic existence is in view. At that point things look hopeful
for us because the ignorance that is the first of the links has
been dramatically weakened. Although we haven't uprooted
it yet, we will not create any new imprints for further cyclic
existence through our actions.

When we have understood emptiness directly, will we
still take rebirth in cyclic existence? Yes, as long as craving and grasping continue to arise. If, however, we are
able to resist responding to feelings with craving, grasping will not occur and the imprints of past actions will not
be activated. This means that the link of existence cannot
occur.

10
**Since formative action is the root
Of cyclic existence, the wise don't act,
But the unwise are agents—
Not the wise because they see suchness.**

Ignorance prevents us from seeing reality as it is and causes us to perceive it in a distorted way, but it is the formative action we perform as a result of this ignorance that is primarily responsible for our continued rebirth. Here, Nagarjuna says that the wise, who have directly experienced reality as it is and are therefore exalted beings, do not perform actions that perpetuate cyclic existence because ignorance can no longer govern what they do. But ordinary beings, who have not understood suchness directly and are not wise with regard to reality, continue to create such actions.

The direct understanding of reality is the result of first gaining a sound intellectual understanding through repeated analysis. We must then familiarize ourselves with what we have established and eventually we will gain a direct experience of reality. From that point onwards the antidote to the misconception of reality has such strength that the misconception cannot act as a motivating force. Imagine a very strong wrestler holding down a much weaker one.

An example of an action motivated by ignorance that does not set off another cycle of the twelve links is one whose results will be experienced in this life. If we perform a very powerful action, its consequences will occur in this very lifetime and it will not act as a cause for a future rebirth. Nor is every action, motivated by ignorance, that ripens in the next or some future lifetime necessarily a formative action. For instance, we may perform actions that express generosity or patience. Though not projecting actions, they can determine what we experience in a future human rebirth: abundant resources as a result of generosity; an attractive appearance and the kind of companions we desire as a result of patience. These are completing actions that complete the conditions of our human existence. The projecting actions decide the kind of rebirth we take, but a variety of other actions will ripen at the same time, creating the circumstances of that life and determining whether we have the potential to live long or enjoy good health and prosperity.

Thus there are three categories of action here: the formative or projecting actions that shape the identity of the next rebirth, namely the kind of body and mind we will have; the accomplishing actions that constitute the tenth link, existence, and make that body and mind come into being; and the completing actions that establish the conditions of that particular life and how much happiness and suffering we experience. The completing actions are not mentioned in this chain of twelve links.

We can take the example of a wall painting. First the outline for the whole painting is drawn. This is like the function of projecting actions. Accomplishing actions are like the execution of the painting through the addition of the color and detail. Other elements, such as the kind of brushes and pigments that are available and the expertise of the painter, determine whether the painting turns out well or not. These factors influence the quality of the outcome, rather like the completing actions.

Even as ordinary people our actions are not all motivated by ignorance and only actions under the strong influence of ignorance create more cyclic existence. Exalted beings may still act out of ignorance, but that ignorance will not dominate them nor produce formative action. The wrestler who is being held down by a strong opponent may still be kicking but is unable to get up. Similarly, ignorance is still present, but the antidote is strong enough to prevent it from taking over.

Ordinary people are dominated by ignorance but it doesn't manifest all the time. However, when it does, unlike exalted beings, we are powerless to counteract it effectively. In our case ignorance is not active when, for instance, we think deeply about the fundamental nature of things. The mental factor of intention is present as one of the five omnipresent factors accompanying our contemplation of reality and it constitutes mental activity. When we feel antipathy towards cyclic existence and with a strong urge for liberation make prostrations, perform a generous action, practice patience, or maintain ethical discipline, these actions are not motivated by ignorance but are actions concordant with liberation.[57]

In his *Great Treatise on the Stages of the Path* Je Tsong-khapa says that, except for actions performed in relation to very special objects through which we accumulate much merit, actions not supported by a wish for freedom from cyclic existence, by the wish to attain enlightenment for the sake of all living beings, or by the correct understanding of reality will all contribute to further cyclic existence.

However, if we could create the virtue necessary for liberation and enlightenment only by having a genuine, constantly present wish to get out of cyclic existence, or the real fully fledged spirit of enlightenment, or a profound understanding of emptiness, it would be very difficult to move from creating the sort of virtue that results in good rebirths within cyclic existence to the kind that gives rise to liberation and enlightenment.

We should not feel discouraged but should remember the story about the Buddha's aged disciple who wanted to become a monk. Even Shariputra, who possessed all kinds of extraordinary powers, could not see in him any virtue that would help his attainment of liberation. The Buddha, however, saw that, without the intention to do so, Shrijata had previously created such virtue. In a past life as a fly he had alighted on some animal droppings and was swept round a stupa by water during a rainstorm. Of course, there was still much to do before he could attain liberation, but his unintentional journey around the stupa had been the beginning. This is what is meant by the power of a special object, here a stupa, which is a structure containing precious relics.

If this is sufficient, then when we consciously arouse the intention, even for a few moments, to free ourselves from cyclic existence or to attain enlightenment for the sake of living beings, or we remind ourselves that things lack inherent existence and then do something virtuous, we must be creating causes for liberation and enlightenment. I strongly believe this, which is why it is worth paying attention to our motivation.

We are fortunate to be able to create much virtue in relation to special objects because we have relatively easy access to great teachers, holy images, and sacred places. We also have the mental capacity to create a positive motivation and arouse feelings of faith. The way we think is all-important. Whether actions we perform are virtuous or not depends on our attitude. Whether or not they become causes for further cyclic existence or for liberation also depends on our intention. The same applies to whether a particular action acts as a cause for just personal liberation or for complete enlightenment. This is why we should make the effort to arouse positive states of mind. Not all actions we perform project further cyclic existence, but we should remember that as humans, more than other creatures, we also have the power to cause ourselves and others serious harm.

Though we may have the wish for freedom from cyclic existence, we cannot fail to realize that it will take time to accomplish and that we will need a succession of good rebirths in which we have the conditions necessary for practice. In order to insure this we may maintain ethical discipline and so forth. These actions will lead to another rebirth and although they may resemble those belonging to the twelve-part process, they are not formative actions but in fact counteract cyclic existence. This shows the importance of changing our way of thinking. In a single moment our mind can do what is very significant and has far-reaching effects.

If the ten virtuous actions, which consist of active restraint from the ten harmful ones, are accompanied by a strong wish for liberation from cyclic existence, they become true paths of insight and will not act as causes for further cyclic existence. If they are accompanied by the spirit of enlightenment, they become causes for complete enlightenment, the very antithesis of our present condition. But they can act as true sources of suffering when they are not accompanied by that wish for freedom, the spirit of enlightenment, or the understanding of reality. In other words, though virtuous, they can be formative actions.

In the *Great Treatise on the Stages of the Path* Je Tsongkhapa says that when we are training ourselves in any of the perfections, for instance in generosity, we should make sure that we practice all the other five perfections—in this case ethical discipline, patience, enthusiastic effort, concentration, and wisdom—and the six excellent factors.[58] When we perform a generous action, ethical discipline will be included if we take care to refrain from doing anything unethical at the same time. In certain situations, for instance, we may be tempted to speak harshly or condescendingly as we give.

Generosity gives rise to abundance, and by insuring that our practice is complete, we create the right environment to use these resources constructively. Sometimes when we give, people respond ungratefully. If we can resist getting upset, we are practicing patience. Giving not out of a sense of obligation or reluctantly nor with a wish to outdo others but with joy is the practice of enthusiastic effort. Directing our full attention to an act of generosity is concentration. Discerning and understanding what is appropriate to give and what is not, and remembering that the giver, the act of generosity, and the recipient are all interdependent and empty of inherent existence are the practice of wisdom. Including these different factors in our actions will bring many excellent results such as a good body and mind, the resources we need, a pleasant appearance, supportive companions, the ability to complete what we undertake, and the focus not to be distracted by the disturbing emotions and so forth. This is how to insure that we will enjoy many conducive conditions in a future human life. On the other hand, our miserliness or impatience now could make us face many difficult circumstances in the future.

Our present human rebirth is the result of ethical actions, but the happiness and suffering each of us experiences is the result of our completing actions. Nevertheless, things are not rigidly predetermined, and we have the freedom to create actions now that will bear positive fruits in this very life. On the simplest level, looking after our health will give us a feeling of well-being and enable us to live out our complete life span, while involvement in substance abuse will shorten our life even though the life span our previous actions projected may have been relatively long. We have the freedom to make choices.

12 Reversing the Process

Whether or not we continue to suffer in cyclic existence depends on whether we perform formative actions. The purified side of the twelve links begins when we become exalted beings with direct experience of reality. Since this stops the creation of formative actions, their imprints will not be left on our consciousness. Even though pleasure and pain are still experienced, we will not respond to these feelings and sensations with craving, thereby preventing grasping and existence, which in turn will preclude rebirth. This is how we contemplate the purified side of the twelve links in forward sequence.

11
When ignorance has stopped
Formative action will not occur.
Ignorance is stopped by awareness
Meditating on suchness.

Only understanding the suchness or fundamental nature of dependently arising phenomena can stop our ignorance. First we must learn about reality and then think about and familiarize ourselves with it until we gain a direct experience.

12
Through the stopping of that, then that,
That and that will not manifest.
The exclusively painful aggregates
Cease to exist in this way.

Stopping one link stops the next, and for a practitioner who can prevent the links from following one upon the other, these exclusively painful aggregates, which are in no way associated with true happiness, will not occur. If a body and mind of this kind do not come into existence again, the suffering associated with them also will not arise. To stop the suffering of death, we have to stop birth and everything that gives rise to birth. And so we retrace our steps back to the stopping of the first link, ignorance.

When we go back from stopping the most critical suffering of death to stopping ignorance, we understand that true cessation of suffering, the third of the noble truths, is possible. When we look at the purified process in forward sequence, namely how stopping ignorance stops formative action and so forth, we understand the true paths of insight that are necessary to bring about cessation of suffering.

In the twenty-sixth chapter of his *Treatise on the Middle Way* Nagarjuna explains the conventional way in which the twelve links chain us to cyclic existence and how we can free ourselves. All the other chapters of his great work are about negating the true existence of the self and other phenomena.[59] He does not mention this theme in the twenty-sixth chapter because he has already conclusively refuted existence of this kind, and it is therefore clear that none of these links could exist in that way. From the ultimate point of view each of these links, like everything clsc that exists, is empty of true or objective existence. Understanding this is crucial for breaking out of the cycle.

The selflessness of persons and the selflessness of other phenomena are about our own lack of intrinsic existence as well as the lack of intrinsic existence of our bodies and minds. When we start to understand the fundamental nature of things, our confusion gradually decreases and we no longer act under its compulsion. As human beings we can think about this. It is said there is no other door to peace, so if we want to pacify our suffering, we must understand the nature of reality. When emptiness is mentioned, we shouldn't immediately think, "This is too complicated for me," and turn away from it.

There are two things to consider: how the self is a dependently existent phenomenon and how other phenomena, particularly our body and mind, are also dependently existent. Focusing on our body and mind, we distort what is there and see them and the self as having true or inherent existence. The fabrication created by this instinctive misconception is the object of negation. Logic allows us to investigate whether how we perceive ourselves is correct or not. The reasoning that conclusively demonstrates the nonexistence of what we fabricate is that the person and other phenomena exist in dependence on a host of different factors.

If we look thoroughly for something we have lost and still cannot find it, we know for certain that it isn't there. First we must identify quite clearly what it is we are searching for. If the self existed in the way our conception apprehends it, we should be able to find it. If despite rigorous investigation we do not, we can be absolutely sure that the self as we perceive it does not exist. In the Buddha's teaching and in the great commentaries many different approaches are explained for gaining this essential understanding and negating the existence of the self that we fabricate. These approaches are intended to stop our instinctive or innate misconception.

Although in this presentation we have gone through the twelve links a number of times both in detail and in summary, which may at first glance appear repetitive, each time new elements were introduced. This is to help us to become familiar with the topic. If as we read or listen to teachings we understand what is said, precious imprints are laid down, even if afterwards we cannot remember all the details. Thinking about what we have learned again and again establishes those imprints firmly.

Understanding of the twelve links is important whether we are seeking a good rebirth, freedom from cyclic existence, or complete enlightenment for the sake of all living beings, but it will only be fruitful if it is supported by the creation of bountiful merit.

13 A GIFT FOR A KING

During the Buddha's lifetime there was a king called Bimbisara[60] who, it is said, struck up a relationship with another
king called Utrayana. Utrayana lived in a rather remote place
and, although the two kings had never met, messengers went
back and forth between them. On one occasion King Utrayana sent King Bimbisara a very precious and special jewel. It
had the power to give a feeling of well-being and to remove
poison when touched.

Since the jewel was priceless, this gift proved quite
an embarrassment to King Bimbisara, who felt obliged to
send a gift of equal value. His ministers tried to estimate the
value of the jewel, but when they calculated it in gold coins,
it turned out to be ten million. How could they reciprocate
with a gift worth ten million gold coins? They could think
of no solution. King Bimbisara was despondent and retired
to a darkened room. He took off his normal finery and lay
down on his bed. Seeing this, one of his ministers, who was
a Brahmin, suggested to the king that he should consult the
Buddha.

The Buddha's advice was simple: he told Bimbisara to
send King Utrayana a painting of himself, the Buddha. A
number of painters were summoned and it was decided that
the best painting would be chosen as the gift. Some versions

96 How Karma Works

of the story recount that when the painters saw the Buddha, they could not stop gazing at him and were quite unable to begin painting. This once again depressed King Bimbisara, but the Buddha solved the problem by using his radiance to project his image onto their canvases. Other accounts say that the Buddha's radiance was so powerful that the painters were dazzled and could not paint him, so he told them to look at his reflection in a pool.

The best image was chosen and the Buddha instructed the painter to depict the twelve links of dependent arising around the edge of the painting. Some verses about this twelve-part process were written at the bottom. The painting was wrapped in many layers of costly silks and brocades. It was carefully placed in a golden box and dispatched to the king, but it was preceded by a letter to him.

The letter announced to King Utrayana that King Bimbisara was sending him a gift that transcended all other gifts in the world. In order to receive it properly he should prepare the road leading to his city and palace by having it cleaned for several miles, and that he and his retinue should welcome it with great ceremony and offerings.

When King Utrayana saw this letter, he felt irritated and insulted by its tone of command, and he remarked to his ministers that he would prepare his troops for battle. But the ministers, who were rather more circumspect and sensible, suggested that it might be a wiser policy first to see what the gift was and then, if it didn't please the king, they could make ready for war. So preparations were made to receive the gift in the manner described by King Bimbisara.

They escorted it ceremonially into the palace. Then, with the whole court waiting in suspense, it was taken out of the golden box. To everyone's surprise, when the many layers of silk and brocade had been removed, what lay before them was a rolled-up painting. Eagerly they unrolled it and found a beautiful portrait of someone they did not know. Present at court, however, were some merchants who had visited Magadha, the area where Bimbisara lived, and they recognized that it was a painting of the Buddha. At once they began speaking words in praise of the Buddha and paid homage to him. King Utrayana and his court had already been prepared for something exceptional. Moved by the image and by the reverence of the merchants, they were quite overcome.

Through the arrival of this gift past positive imprints were awakened in the king and his court. The king took the painting to his private quarters. That evening he looked carefully at the twelve images around the edge and read the verses. Throughout the night he thought very deeply about this whole twelve-part process in forward and reverse sequence, and in the course of this intensive meditation he reached the stage of a stream enterer,[61] that is, he had direct perception of the truth. It is said that even just seeing these twelve links depicted creates beneficial imprints, so thinking about them again and again with understanding of how they function will undoubtedly have a very profound effect and bring vast benefit.

The *King of Meditative Stabilizations Sutra*[62] says that even if we look at the image of a Buddha when we are angry, negativity created over many aeons is purified. If that is true, we can easily imagine how much negativity is purified and how much virtue created when we look at such an image with faith in our hearts, make a gesture of homage as an expression of that faith and speak words of praise. The four noble truths, the twelve links of dependent arising and the two truths regarding conventional and ultimate reality, all interrelated, form the very core of the Buddha's teaching. The many different practices of sutra and tantra become meaningful and purposeful only when they are based on a good understanding of these fundamental and seminal principles.

APPENDIX 1
CONTENTS OF NAGARJUNA'S *TREATISE ON THE MIDDLE WAY*

This presentation is based on Je Tsongkhapa's *Ocean of Reasoning, Explanation of (Nagarjuna's) "Treatise on the Middle Way."*[63] The order in which Je Tsongkhapa presents the contents has been retained.

CHAPTER 18
By examining the self and phenomena (*bdag dang chos brtag pa*) this chapter establishes that the self and what pertains to the self, as conceived by ignorance, do not exist.

CHAPTER 2
Such a refutation could give rise to the thought that there is no self that comes from a previous life and goes to a future life and that there is no one who creates actions and experiences their results. To counter this the second chapter examines coming and going (*'gro 'ong brtag pa*) as well as actions and agents.

CHAPTER 9
To rebut the idea that if nothing is inherently existent, there

is no one who takes on the aggregates, the ninth chapter examines whether the one who experiences exists prior (*snga rol na gnas pa brtag pa*) to that which is experienced.

CHAPTER 10
Examples and proofs are adduced to establish the inherent existence of the one who takes on the aggregates. Their validity is refuted in the tenth chapter by examining fire and fuel (*me dang bud shing brtag pa*) to show that mutual dependence does not establish inherent existence but precludes it.

CHAPTER 11
The Buddha spoke of the beginningless and endless nature of cyclic existence. To refute assertions that because there is cyclic existence there must be someone in cyclic existence, because there is suffering there must be someone who is suffering, and that there could be continuity only if this person were inherently existent, the eleventh chapter examines the former and later limits (*sngon dang phyi ma'i mtha' brtag pa*).

CHAPTER 12
The twelfth chapter examines how suffering arises and whether it is produced from that which is of the same nature or from that which is of a different nature (*bdag dang gzhan gyi byas pa brtag pa*).

CHAPTER 1
The first chapter examines conditions (*rkyen brtag pa*), refuting the inherent existence of production with respect to internal and external phenomena in order to refute a self of phenomena.

CHAPTERS 3, 4, 5
The Buddha spoke of the aggregates, sources, and constituents as the basis for the misconception of a self of phenomena. To refute the idea that they are inherently existent the third chapter examines the faculties (*dbang po brtag pa*); the fourth examines the aggregates (*phung po brtag pa*); and the fifth examines the constituents (*khams brtag pa*).

CHAPTER 6
The sixth chapter examines desire and the desirous person or mind (*'dod chags dang chags pa brtag pa*), which depend on the aggregates, sources, and constituents.

CHAPTER 7
The seventh chapter examines production, duration, and disintegration (*skye gnas 'jig gsum brtag pa*), the attributes of products.

CHAPTER 8
The eighth chapter, which examines agents and actions (*byed pa po dang las brtag pa*), is a refutation of the inherent existence of both persons and other phenomena.

CHAPTER 13
By examining products (*'du byed brtag pa*) the thirteenth chapter demonstrates that functional things are empty of inherent existence, without making any distinction between persons and other phenomena.

CHAPTERS 14, 15, 16
Proponents of inherent existence assert that whether or not distinctions between persons and other phenomena are made, their inherent existence is proven by the fact that things meet or come together; by the fact that there are causes and con-

ditions; and by the fact that there is cyclic existence with one rebirth following another. To counter these ideas the fourteenth chapter examines meeting (*phrad pa brtag pa*); the fifteenth examines nature (*rang bzhin brtag pa*); the sixteenth examines bondage and freedom (*bcings pa dang thar pa brtag pa*).

CHAPTER 17
The seventeenth chapter examines actions and their effects (*las brtag pa*) to refute the idea that cyclic existence is inherently existent because it is the basis for the relationship between actions and their effects.

CHAPTER 19
The nineteenth chapter examines time (*dus brtag pa*) to refute the assumption that functional things are inherently existent because they act as the basis for the designation of past, present, and future.

CHAPTER 20
The twentieth chapter examines aggregations (*tshogs pa brtag pa*) in order to refute the notion that time is inherently existent because it acts as a cooperative or contributing condition for the arising of an effect and is a cause for its coming into existence and disintegration.

CHAPTER 21
It is asserted that the continuum of worldly existence cannot be empty of inherent existence because there are Those Thus Gone, Tathagatas, who have put an end to the continuum of their own worldly existence and because there are disturbing attitudes and emotions which act as the source of that continuum. To refute these ideas the twenty-first chapter examines origination and disintegration (*'byung ba dang 'jig pa brtag pa*).

CHAPTER 22

The twenty-second chapter refutes these ideas by examining Tathagatas (*de bzhin gshegs pa brtag pa*).

CHAPTER 23

The twenty-third chapter examines that which is distorted (*phyin ci log brtag pa*), such as holding what is impermanent to be unchanging.

CHAPTER 24

The argument is put forward that if all phenomena were empty, the four noble truths would not be feasible. The twenty-fourth chapter examines the four noble truths (*'phags pa'i bden pa brtag pa*) to demonstrate that where there is absence of inherent existence everything is feasible, whereas the converse would be true if things were inherently existent.

CHAPTER 25

To refute the idea that the state beyond sorrow, nirvana, is not feasible if things are empty of inherent existence, the twenty-fifth chapter examines the state beyond sorrow (*mya ngan las 'das pa brtag pa*).

CHAPTER 26

The Buddha taught that dependent arising and the middle way mean the same thing. Ignorance with regard to the suchness which has been described in the preceding chapters insures continued involvement in cyclic existence, but through dispelling that ignorance the process can be brought to an end. For this purpose the twenty-sixth chapter examines the twelve links of existence (*srid pa yan lag bcu gnyis brtag pa*).

CHAPTER 27
To show that understanding the suchness of dependent arising will prevent one from clinging to misleading views, such
as those relating to a beginning or to an end, the twenty-sev-
enth chapter examines views (*lta ba brtag pa*).

APPENDIX 2

WAYS OF SUMMARIZING THE TWELVE LINKS

In Nagarjuna's text the twelve links are presented in forward sequence. They can be summarized in four different ways.

1   In terms of that which projects and what is projected, followed by that which accomplishes and what is accomplished: Ignorance, formative action, and consciousness project name and form, the six sources, contact, and feeling. Craving, grasping, and existence accomplish birth and aging and death.

2   In terms of true suffering and true sources of suffering: Ignorance, formative action, craving, grasping, and existence are all true sources of suffering. Of these, two—formative action and existence—are action, while the rest are disturbing attitudes and emotions. Consciousness, name and form, the six sources, contact, feeling, birth, and aging and death constitute true suffering.

3   In terms of three aspects of the afflicted side of
    phenomena[64]—disturbing attitudes and emotions,
    action, and suffering: Ignorance, craving, and grasping
    are disturbing attitudes and emotions; formative action
    and existence are contaminated action; name and form,
    the six sources, contact, feeling, consciousness, birth,
    and aging and death constitute suffering.

4   In terms of causes and effects: The first, second, and
    third links are the projecting causes, while the fourth
    to the seventh links are their effects. The eighth, ninth,
    and tenth links are the accomplishing causes and the
    eleventh and twelfth links are their effects.

The actual projecting cause is formative action. Ignorance
is causal because it motivates the action, and consciousness
is causal since it serves as the seedbed for the imprint. The
projected effects can be classed as that which forms the identity of the five aggregates and that which is associated with
experience. Name and form establish the bare identity and
the six sources establish the attributes, at which point an experiencer has come into existence. Contact constitutes experience of the object and causes experience of a maturation by
feeling. This refers to the experience of the results of past actions in the form of happiness or suffering and includes both
what is being experienced and the act of experiencing. When
there is contact through the coming together of an object,
a sense faculty, and a consciousness, the ability to discern
whether the object is pleasant, unpleasant, or neutral occurs.
Experiencing the object refers to the ability to differentiate
in this way, which induces pleasurable, painful, or neutral
feelings.

The main accomplishing cause is existence. Craving and
grasping give rise to this. What is accomplished is birth,

while aging and death are the drawbacks of having been born. Considering the twelve links in these different ways helps us to become more closely acquainted with the process.

THE ROOT TEXT

EXAMINING THE TWELVE LINKS OF EXISTENCE

1   Obscured by ignorance, existence recurs
    From performing any of the three kinds
    Of formative actions through which
    One goes on to another rebirth.

2   Conditioned by formative action,
    Consciousness enters rebirths.
    When consciousness has entered,
    Name and form come into being.

3   When name and form have come into being,
    The six sources emerge.
    In dependence on these six sources
    Contact properly arises.

4   It arises only through the eye,
    A form, and that which remembers.
    Therefore consciousness arises
    In dependence on name and form.

5   Contact is a combination of three—
Eye, form, and consciousness—
And from such contact
Feeling always arises.

6   Conditioned by feeling there is craving
And the craving is for feeling.
Whenever there is this craving
Grasping of four kinds arises.

7   When there is grasping, existence
Of the one who grasps occurs.
When there is no grasping, one is freed
And will not come into existence.

8   Existence, moreover, is the five aggregates.
Through existence birth occurs.
Aging, death, and sorrow,
Lamentation and suffering,

9   Unhappiness and distress
All come from being born.
Thus these exclusively painful
Aggregates come into being.

10   Since formative action is the root
Of cyclic existence, the wise don't act,
But the unwise are agents—
Not the wise because they see suchness.

11   When ignorance has stopped
Formative action will not occur.
Ignorance is stopped by awareness
Meditating on suchness.

12 Through the stopping of that, then that,
That and that will not manifest.
The exclusively painful aggregates
Cease to exist in this way.

THE TIBETAN TEXT

༡ མ་རིག་བསྐྱེབས་པས་ཡང་སྲིད་ཕྱིར།
འདུ་བྱེད་རྣམ་པ་གསུམ་པོ་དག།
མངོན་པར་འདུ་བྱེད་གང་ཡིན་པའི།
ལས་དེ་དག་གྱིས་འགྲོ་བར་འགྲོ།

༢ འདུ་བྱེད་རྐྱེན་ཅན་རྣམ་པར་ཤེས།
འགྲོ་བ་རྣམས་སུ་འཇུག་པར་འགྱུར།
རྣམ་པར་ཤེས་པ་ཞུགས་གྱུར་ན།
མིང་དང་གཟུགས་ནི་ཆགས་པར་འགྱུར།

༣ མིང་དང་གཟུགས་ནི་ཆགས་གྱུར་ན།
སྐྱེ་མཆེད་དྲུག་ནི་འབྱུང་བར་འགྱུར།
སྐྱེ་མཆེད་དྲུག་ལ་བརྟེན་ནས་ནི།
རེག་པ་ཡང་དག་འབྱུང་བར་འགྱུར།

113

༥   མིག་དང་གཟུགས་དང་དུན་བྱེད་ལ།
བརྟེན་ནས་སྐྱེ་བ་ཁོ་ན་སྟེ།
དེ་ལྟར་མིང་དང་གཟུགས་བརྟེན་ནས
རྣམ་པར་ཤེས་པ་སྐྱེ་བར་འགྱུར།

༦   མིག་དང་གཟུགས་དང་རྣམ་པར་ཤེས།
གསུམ་པོ་འདུས་པ་གང་ཡིན་པ།
དེ་ནི་རེག་པའོ་རེག་དེ་ལས།
ཚོར་བ་ཀུན་ཏུ་འབྱུང་བར་འགྱུར།

༧   ཚོར་བའི་རྐྱེན་གྱིས་སྲེད་པ་སྟེ།
ཚོར་བའི་དོན་དུ་སྲེད་པར་འགྱུར།
སྲེད་པར་གྱུར་ན་ཉེ་བར་ལེན།
རྣམ་པ་བཞི་པོ་ཉེར་ལེན་འགྱུར།

v   ཉེར་ལེན་ཡོད་ན་ལེན་པ་པོའི།
སྲིད་པ་རབ་ཏུ་འབྱུང་བར་འགྱུར།
གལ་ཏེ་ཉེ་བར་ལེན་མེད་ན།
གྲོལ་བར་འགྱུར་ཏེ་སྲིད་མི་འགྱུར།

༨ སྙིད་པ་དེ་ཡང་ཕུང་པོ་ལྷ།
སྙིད་པ་ལས་ནི་སྐྱེ་བར་འགྱུར།
རྒྱུ་ཡི་དང་ནི་སྐུ་ངན་དང་།
སྐྱེ་སྲུགས་འདོན་བཅས་སྲུག་བསྲལ་དང་།

༩ ཡིད་མི་བདེ་དང་འཁྲུག་པ་རྣམས།
དེ་དག་སྐྱེ་ལས་རབ་ཏུ་འབྱུང་།
དེ་ལྟར་སྲུག་བསྲལ་ཕུང་པོ་ནི།
འབའ་ཞིག་པ་འདི་འབྱུང་བར་འགྱུར།

༡༠ འགོར་བའི་རྩ་བ་འདུ་བྱེད་དེ།
དེ་ཕྱིར་མཁས་རྣམས་འདུ་མི་བྱེད།
དེ་ཕྱིར་མི་མཁས་བྱེད་པོ་ཡིན།
མཁས་མིན་དེ་ཉིད་མཐོང་ཕྱིར་རོ།

༡༡ མ་རིག་འགགས་པར་གྱུར་ན་ནི།
འདུ་བྱེད་རྣམས་ཀྱང་འབྱུང་མི་འགྱུར།
མ་རིག་འགག་པ་ར་འགྱུར་བ་ནི།
ཤེས་པས་དེ་ཉིད་བསྐོམས་པས་སོ།

༢༢　དེ་དང་དེ་ནི་འགགས་གྱུར་པས།
དེ་དང་དེ་ནི་མངོན་མི་འབྱུང་།
སྤྲུག་བསྒྲལ་ཕུང་པོ་འབའ་ཞིག་པ།
དེ་ནི་དེ་ལྟར་ཡང་དག་འགག།

རྩ་བ་ཤེས་རབ་ལས་སྲིད་པའི་ཡན་ལག་བཅུ་གཉིས་བརྟག་པ་ཞེས་བྱ་བ་སྟེ་
རབ་ཏུ་བྱེད་པ་ཉི་ཤུ་རྩུག་པའོ།།

NOTES

Abbreviation:
P: *Tibetan Tripiṭaka* (Tokyo-Kyoto: Tibetan Tripiṭaka Research Foundation, 1956)

1. The twelve links of dependent arising (*rten 'brel yan lag bcu gnyis*) are normally enumerated in the following order: (1) ignorance (*ma rig pa*), (2) formative action (*'du byed kyi las*), (3) consciousness (*rnam par shes pa*), (4) name and form (*ming gzugs*), (5) the sources (*skyed mched*), (6) contact (*reg pa*), (7) feeling (*tshor ba*), (8) craving (*sred pa*), (9) grasping (*len pa*), (10) existence (*srid pa*), (11) birth (*skye ba*), and (12) aging and death (*rga shi*).

2. In the desire realm (*'dod khams*), to which our world belongs, preoccupation with the objects of the senses is the driving force. The gods of the form and formless realms (*gzugs khams, gzugs med khams*) are absorbed in deep states of concentration and experience subtle pleasurable or neutral feelings as a result of this.

3. The five aggregates (*phung po lnga*) are form (*gzugs kyi phung po*), feeling (*tshor ba'i phung po*), recognition (*'du shes kyi phung po*), compositional factors (*'du byed kyi*

117

phung po), and consciousness (*rnam shes kyi phung po*). All products can be included in the five aggregates and may be classified as those with or without form. The aggregate of form includes everything that we perceive through our senses: sights, sounds, smells, tastes, and tactile sensations. Feeling is a mental function or factor consisting of pleasurable, painful, or neutral physical or mental experience. Discrimination is the mental function that allows us to identify and differentiate between things. Consciousness refers to the five kinds of sense consciousness and mental consciousness. All other mental activity falls into the aggregate of compositional factors. This also includes such things as a year, a day, time, and the person. The fourth aggregate is vast.

Since feeling and discrimination are both mental functions, why are they set apart as separate aggregates and not simply included in the fourth aggregate? Feelings and different kinds of discrimination form a basis for conflict. Lay people experience conflict in their pursuit of pleasurable feelings and sensations through involvement with the objects of the senses. In trying to look after those close to them, attachment and antipathy give rise to pleasurable and painful feelings that easily lead to conflict. Conflict may also arise through attachment to views and ideologies, which are different forms of discrimination.

4. The Mahayana or Great Vehicle (*theg pa chen po*) consists of the causal Perfection Vehicle (*rgyu pha rol tu chin pa'i theg pa*) and the resultant Secret Mantra Vehicle (*'bras bu gsang sngags kyi theg pa*). The Perfection Vehicle is the body of practices described in the Mahayana sutras by which over three incalculably long aeons a Bodhisattva creates the great stores of merit and insight necessary for enlightenment. The Secret Mantra Vehicle consists of the practices described in the tantras through which enlightenment can

be attained in one short lifetime. These practices are suitable for practitioners of the very highest caliber. By virtue of simulating the desired result, enlightenment, through tantric practice, the result actually comes into being.

5. The Indian master Nagarjuna (Klu sgrub, first to second century) was the trailblazer who established the Madhyamika or middle way system of philosophical tenets which propound that while nothing has true existence, the conventional existence of actions and agents is feasible. His most famous work, the *Treatise on the Middle Way* (*Madhyamakaśāstra, dBu ma'i bstan bcos*, P5224, Vol. 95), also called *Fundamental Wisdom* (*Mūlamadhyamaka, rTsa ba shes rab*), is a work in twenty-seven chapters which presents the explicit content of the Perfection of Wisdom Sutras. It emphasizes dependent arising and explains the paths of insight related to the understanding of emptiness, employing a wide variety of approaches and lines of reasoning. For the contents of Nagarjuna's *Treatise*, see Appendix 1. English translation: Jay L. Garfield, *The Fundamental Wisdom of the Middle Way* (New York: Oxford University Press, 1995).

6. The Indian master Chandrakirti (Zla ba grags pa, seventh century) was one of the main spiritual heirs of Nagarjuna, whose works on sutra and tantra he elucidated and propagated. He lived in the monastic university of Nalanda and was an accomplished practitioner. Chandrakirti's *Supplement to the Middle Way* (*Madhyamakāvatāra, dBu ma la 'jug pa*, P5261, P5262, Vol. 98) is a commentary on the meaning of Nagarjuna's *Treatise on the Middle Way*, which it supplements with regard to both the profound and extensive aspects of practice. It deals with the ten Bodhisattva stages. English translation: C.W. Huntington, Jr. and Geshé Namgyal Wangchen, *The Emptiness of Emptiness: An Introduction to*

Early Indian Mādhyamika (Honolulu: University of Hawai'i Press, 1989).

7. The Indian master Shantideva (Zhi ba lha) lived in the monastic university of Nalanda during the eighth century. To others he appeared quite unaccomplished and they said he only knew three things: how to eat, sleep, and defecate. In an attempt to humiliate him he was designated to teach before a large gathering. To everyone's amazement he showed himself to be a very great master by teaching his guide to the Bodhisattva way of life, the *Way of the Bodhisattva* (*Bodhisattvacaryāvatāra, Byang chub sems dpa'i spyod pa la 'jug pa*, P5272, Vol. 99). English translations: *A Guide to the Bodhisattva's Way of Life*, Stephen Batchelor, trans. (Dharamsala: Library of Tibetan Works and Archives, 1979); *The Bodhicaryavatara*, Kate Crosby and Andrew Skilton, trans. (Oxford: Oxford University Press, 1995); *A Guide to the Bodhisattva Way of Life*, Vesna A. Wallace and B. Alan Wallace, trans. (Ithaca: Snow Lion Publications, 1997); *The Way of the Bodhisattva*, Padmakara Translation Group, trans. (Boston: Shambhala Publications, 1997).

8. The spirit of enlightenment (*byang chub kyi sems*) has two aspects: the conventional spirit of enlightenment (*kun rdzob byang chub kyi sems*), which is the consciousness accompanying the intention to become enlightened for the sake of all living beings; and the ultimate spirit of enlightenment (*don dam byang chub kyi sems*), which is the direct understanding of reality, namely that all phenomena are empty of inherent existence, supported by this intention.

9. The practices of giving (*sbyin pa*), ethical discipline (*tshul khrims*), patience (*bzod pa*), enthusiastic effort (*brtson 'grus*), concentration (*bsam gtan*), and wisdom (*shes rab*)

become perfections and practices of Bodhisattvas when the intention underlying them is the altruistic wish to become enlightened for the sake of all living beings. The first five are said to be like a group of blind people who cannot reach the destination of enlightenment without the last, wisdom, which is like their sighted guide. Concentration and wisdom are more easily practiced by ordained people than by lay people. Those who live the life of a householder, however, have plenty of opportunities to practice the first three perfections. Whether lay or ordained, it is important to develop enthusiastic effort, which is a delight in virtue.

10. See the section entitled "The Selfless" in Jeffrey Hopkins's *Meditation on Emptiness* (London: Wisdom Publications, 1983) for a concise presentation of products and non-products.

11.   *rten cing 'brel bar 'byung ba gang*
       de ni stong pa nyid du bshad
       de ni brten nas gdags pa ste
       de ni dbu ma'i lam yin no

       gang phyir rten 'byung ma yin pa'i
       chos 'ga' yod pa ma yin pa
       de phyir stong pa ma yin pa'i
       chos 'ga' yod pa ma yin no

12. The Indian master Asaṅga (*Thogs med*) lived in the fourth century and was a trailblazer in establishing the Chittamatra (*sems tsam*) system of philosophical tenets, although he himself is said to have held the Prasangika-Madhyamika (*dbu ma thal 'gyur pa*) view. His *Compendium of Knowledge* (*Abhidharmasamuccaya, mNgon pa kun btus*, P5550, Vol. 112) sets out the focal objects of the paths: the aggregates, constituents, and elements; the four noble truths; and the

twelve links of dependent arising. An extensive explanation
of mind and mental activities is included. The text contains
instruction on how to practice by controlling one's senses
and training in ethical discipline, concentration, and wisdom
as well as explanation of the thirty-seven factors concordant
with enlightenment. It concludes by explaining the results
of these practices, through which all faults are brought to
an end and the highest wisdom is attained. These topics are
presented mainly from a Chittamatrin standpoint.

13. *Śālistambasūtra*, P876, Vol. 34. "Because this exists,
that comes into existence/that occurs" (*'di yod pas na 'di
'byung*) indicates the condition of no movement (*mi g.yo
ba'i rkyen*); "because this has been produced, that has been
produced" (*'di skyes ba'i phyir 'di skyes te*) indicates the
condition of impermanence (*mi rtag pa'i rkyen*); and "conditioned by ignorance there is formative action" (*ma rig pa'i
rkyen gyis 'du byed*) indicates the condition of potential (*nus
pa'i rkyen*).

14. (1) They have come from causes (*rgyu dang bcas las
byung ba*). (2) They have come from impermanent conditions
(*mi rtag pa'i rkyen las byung ba*). (3) They are characterized
by selflessness (*bdag med pa'i mtshan nyid*). (4) They have
come from conditions with potential (*nus pa'i rkyen las byung
ba*). (5) They have come from conditions free from [the act of]
creation (*bya ba med pa'i rkyen las byung ba*).

15. *Ci yi phyir rten cing 'brel bar byung ba zhes bya zhe na
smras pa rgyu dang bcas rkyen dang bcas pa la bya yi rgyu
med rkyen med la ni ma yin no.*

16. Je Tsongkhapa (Tsong kha pa Blo bzang grags pa, 1357-
1419), born in Amdo (A mdo), was a great reformer, dedi-

cated practitioner, and prolific writer. He founded Ganden Monastery (dGa' ldan rnam par rgyal ba'i gling) in 1409, the first of the monastic universities of the new Kadampa (bKa' gdams gsar ma) or Gelugpa (dGe lugs pa) tradition. He wrote a number of works on the stages of the path to enlightenment, the longest being his *Lam rim chen mo.* English translation: *The Great Treatise on the Stages of the Path to Enlightenment,* ed. Joshua W. C. Cutler and Guy Newland, 3 vols. (Ithaca, N.Y.: Snow Lion Publications, 2000-2004).

17. The proponents of the four schools of Buddhist philosophical tenets are the Vaibhashikas (*bye brag smra ba*), the Sautrantikas (*mdo sde pa*), the Chittamatrins (*sems tsam pa*), and the Madhyamikas (*dbu ma pa*), consisting of the Svatantrikas (*rang rgyud pa*) and the Prasangikas (*thal 'gyur pa*). See Geshe Lhundup Sopa and Jeffrey Hopkins, *Cutting Through Appearances: Practice and Theory of Tibetan Buddhism* (Ithaca, N.Y.: Snow Lion Publications, 1989) for a succinct presentation of these systems of thought.

18. Partless functional things: *cha med kyi ngos po.*

19. Dependent arising in relation to products does not always imply a cause-and-effect relationship. For instance, the agent of an action is dependent on the action, but the action is not the cause of the agent. Similarly valid cognition and what is cognized, a proof and the probandum, long and short, etc., are dependently arising products but are not causes and effects. For proponents of the Prasangika school not only do effects depend upon the causes that produce them, but causes depend on their effects, inasmuch as they can only be posited as causes in relation to the effects they produce.

20. Arising or produced in dependence: *rten nas 'byung ba* or *skye ba*; arising or produced through meeting: *phrad nas 'byung ba* or *skye ba*; arising or produced through relationship: *ltos nas 'byung ba* or *skye ba*; arising or existing in dependence: *rten nas 'byung ba* or *grub pa*; arising or existing through meeting: *phrad nas 'byung ba* or *grub pa*; arising or existing through relationship: *ltos nas 'byung ba* or *grub pa*.

21. (1) *byed pa po med pa'i don*, (2) *rgyu dang bcas pa'i don*, (3) *sems can med pa'i don*, (4) *gzhan gyi dbang gis don*, (5) *g.yo wa med pa'i don*, (6) *mi rtag pa'i don*, (7) *skad cig ma'i don*, (8) *rgyu dang 'bras bu rgyun mi chad pa'i don*, (9) *rgyu dang 'bras bu mthun pa'i don*, (10) *rgyu dang 'bras bu sna tshogs pa'i don*, (11) *rgyu dang 'bras bu so sor nges pa'i don*.

22. The afflicted side or the aspect associated with the disturbing attitudes and emotions: *kun nas nyon mongs kyi phyogs*; the purified side: *rnam byang gi phyogs*.

23. Forward sequence: *lugs 'byung*; reverse or backward sequence: *lugs ldog*.

24. *Abridged Stages of the Path*, *Lam rim bsdus don / Byang chub lam gyi rim pa'i nyams len gyi rnam gzhag mdor bsdus*, The Collected Works of Rje Tsoṅ-kha-pa Blo-bzaṅ-grags-pa, Vol. kha, *thor bu*, 65b.2-68b.1 (New Delhi: Ngawang Gelek Demo, 1975).

25. Geshe Puchungwa (Phu chung gZhon nu rgyal mtshan, 1031-1106). The Kadampa (bKa' gdams pa) tradition was founded by Dromtön Gyelway Jungnay ('Brom ston rGyal ba'i 'byung gnas, 1004-1064), a lay practitioner and the main Tibetan disciple of the Indian master Atisha (Dipam-

kara Shrijnana, usually referred to as Jo bo rje in Tibetan, 982-1054). The Kadampa masters were known for their down-to-earth approach to practice, which they presented according to the three levels of capacity explained in Atisha's *Lamp for the Path to Enlightenment (Bodhipathapradīpa, Byang chub lam gyi sgron ma*, P5343, Vol. 103). In public they laid great emphasis on the practice of sutra and kept their personal practice of tantra hidden. They regarded all of the Buddha's words *(bka')* as actual instructions *(gdams)* for practice.

26. People are motivated by different intentions when they practice the Buddha's teachings. From a Buddhist point of view practice of the teachings is considered authentic when it is motivated at least by the wish to gain a good rebirth. A practitioner of the initial level or most limited capacity *(skye bu chung ngu)* engages in practices which make this possible. A practitioner of the intermediate level *(skye bu 'bring)* is concerned with personal liberation from all rebirth within cyclic existence as a result of actions underlain by disturbing attitudes and emotions, and engages in practices which lead to such freedom. A practitioner of the highest level or great capacity *(skye bu chen po)* is motivated by the spirit of enlightenment *(byang chub sems)* and does what is necessary to become a fully enlightened Buddha for the sake of others. Even if from the outset we are motivated by the wish to become fully enlightened in order to help others in the most effective way, we must still gain the insights associated with the initial and intermediate levels, since these insights form the foundation for the practices that are unique to the Great Vehicle.

27. The three nonvirtuous or harmful physical actions are killing *(srog gchod pa)*, stealing *(ma byin par len pa)* and

sexual misconduct (*'dod pas log par g.yem pa*). The four nonvirtuous verbal activities are lying (*rdzun du smra ba*), using divisive language (*phra ma*), using harsh language (*tshig rtsub*), and idle talk (*ngag kyal*). The three nonvirtuous mental activities are covetous thoughts (*brnab sems*), harmful thoughts (*gnod sems*), and wrong views (*log lta*).

28. *skad cig ma'i rten 'brel.*

29. This presentation of the twelve links at different junctures or in different phases (*gnas skabs kyi rten 'brel*) describes a series of critical periods with regard to the five aggregates. The five aggregates at the time of the ignorance that set in motion the action which brought us into this life constitute the link of ignorance. The aggregates when that action was performed are the link of formative action. The aggregates at conception into this life are the link of consciousness. The aggregates from the moment after conception till immediately before the six faculties are fully formed are the link of name and form. The aggregates from when the six faculties are fully functional till just before visual perception and the other kinds of consciousness are able to operate are the link of the six sources. The aggregates from the point where the faculty, its object, and the respective consciousness come together but before pleasurable, painful, or neutral feelings can be discerned are the link of contact. The aggregates from the time when these three kinds of feelings can be experienced until just before sexual union can take place are the link of feeling. The aggregates from the time when sexual union is possible but while a partner is still being sought and sexual union has not yet been experienced are the link of craving. The aggregates during the time of the motivation for the action that will precipitate the next life are the link of grasping. This refers to the period when one is looking for a male or

female with whom to have the sexual intercourse that will be responsible for the next rebirth but before that particular act has been performed. The aggregates at the time of creating the action which leads to the next life are the link of existence. The aggregates at the time of conception into the next life are the link of birth and from the moment after conception until one again has the capability to have sexual intercourse are the twelfth link, aging and death.

This explanation is based on the third chapter of the Indian master Vasubandhu's (dByig gnyen) *Treasury of Knowledge* (*Abhidharmakośa, Chos mngon pa'i mdzod*, P5590, Vol. 115), where he attributes this presentation to certain proponents of the Vaibhashika school of tenets. He writes:

> *ma rig nyon mongs sngon gnas skabs*
> *'du byed dag ni sngon las kyi*
> *rnam shes mtshams sbyor phung po yin*
> *ming dang gzugs ni de phan chad*
> *skye mched drug dod tshun chad do*
> *de ni gsum 'dus tshun chad do*
> *reg pa bde sdug la sogs kyi*
> *rgyu shes nus pa tshun chad do*
> *tshor 'khrig tshun chad sred pa ni*
> *long spyod 'khrig pa chags can gyi*
> *nyer bar len pa long spyod rnams*
> *thob par bya phyir yongs rgyug pa'i*
> *de srid 'bras bu 'byung 'gyur ba'i*
> *las byed de ni srid pa yin*
> *nying mtshams sbyor ba skye ba yin*
> *tshor ba'i bar ni rga shi yin*
> *de ni gnas skabs par 'dod lo*

30. Projecting causes: *'phen byed kyi rgyu*; projected effects: *'phangs 'bras*; accomplishing causes: *'grub byed kyi*

rgyu; accomplished effects: *grub 'bras*. See Appendix 2 for an explanation of the different ways of summarizing the twelve links.

31. *gang tshe rang dbang 'jug cing mthun gnas pa*
    gal te 'di bdag 'dzin par mi byed na
    g.yang sar lhung bas bzhan dbang 'jug 'gyur pa
    de las phyi nas gang gis slong bar 'gyur

32. *gti mug phag pa rmongs gyur bas*
    gtsang ma'i ni gsang grog por gtong
    dag pa'i zhing la yid mi chags
    ma dag shing du dga' bde skyong
    mi gtsang 'dam la rkan sgra tog
    gzhan yang gti mug phag pa nyid
    nges par gsod kyang bdag por 'khrul
    ci thar 'bros par mi rtsom par
    sbang chol slu 'brid zhim zhim za

33. Nonvirtuous actions (*mi dge ba'i las*), contaminated virtuous actions (*zag bcas dge ba'i las*), and unfluctuating actions (*mi g.yo ba'i las*) lead to a rebirth in one of the three realms of cyclic existence. Nonvirtuous actions lead to a rebirth as a hell-being, a hungry spirit or as an animal in the desire realm (*'dod khams*) and virtuous contaminated actions to a rebirth in the same realm as a human or celestial being. Unfluctuating actions lead to rebirth in the form realm (*gzugs khams*) and in the formless realm (*gzugs med khams*). One must have attained a calmly abiding mind (*zhi gnas*) in order to create such actions. There are four concentrations (*bsam gtan*) of the form realm which are differentiated on the basis of the accompanying feelings. A progressive development towards neutral feeling takes place. The form realm has seventeen abodes (*gnas*) divided among these four concentrations.

The four absorptions (*snyoms 'jug*) of the formless realm are called limitless space (*nam mkha' mtha' yas*), limitless consciousness (*rnam shes mtha' yas*), nothingness (*ci yang med*), and the peak of cyclic existence (*srid rtse*). They are diffcrentiated on the basis of the accompanying discrimination, which becomes less and less coarse.

34. The transitory collection (*'jig tshogs*) refers to the body and mind, which undergo constant change and to which the validly existing self is attributed. This self is not perceived as it is but is distorted by the false view.

35. The Indian master Dharmakirti (Chos kyi grags pa) lived in the seventh century. He propagated the Chittamatra view and was an expert in the definition of valid perception, valid scriptural statements, and valid persons. He wrote seven treatises on valid cognition, among them his famous *Commentary on (Dignaga's) "Compendium of Valid Cognition"* (*Pramāṇavārttika, Tshad ma rnam 'grel*, P5709, Vol. 130).

36. The Indian master Bhavaviveka (Legs ldan 'byed) lived in the sixth century. He was born in south India and studied at the monastic foundation at Magadha, close to Bodhgaya. He was a great exponent of Madhyamika philosophy and wrote a famous text called the *Heart of the Middle Way* (*Madhyamukahṛdaya, dBu ma'i snying po*, P5255, Vol. 96). Bhavaviveka also wrote a famous commentary on Nagarjuna's *Treatise on the Middle Way*. The general tenets of the Svatantrika school of Madhyamika philosophy and in particular those of the Sautrantika-Svatantrika branch are based on his writing.

37. The antithesis of ignorance (*ma rig pa*) is the knowledge which correctly understands reality. This is often re-

ferred to as *rikpa yeshe* (*rig pa ye shes*). Although the word *yeshe* is often translated as "exalted wisdom," here it does not necessarily refer to a direct understanding of reality nor to a path of insight, since the latter is necessarily accompanied by a constantly present wish for freedom from cyclic existence.

38. *shes rab nyon mongs can*

39. Je Tsongkhapa's *Praise for Dependent Arising,* also known as the *Short Essence of Eloquence* (*rTen 'grel bstod pa* or *Legs bshad snying po chung ngu*, P6016, Vol. 153), is a praise to the Buddha Shakyamuni for uniquely teaching dependent arising and emptiness. The lines cited here are from an unpublished translation in progress, *Praise for Dependent Relativity*, by Ven. Graham Woodhouse, Institute of Buddhist Dialectics, Dharamsala, India. He explains that he has used the iambic tetrameter and iambic pentameter to imitate the seven- and nine-syllable lines of the original in the hope that the English translation can be chanted as has traditionally been done in Tibetan monasteries which follow the tradition of Je Tsongkhapa. For another translation, see *The Key to the Treasury of Shunyata*, by Sermey Khensur Lobsang Tarchin (Howell, NJ: Mahayana Sutra and Tantra Press, 2002).

40. In his *Compendium of Knowledge* Asanga describes fifty-one secondary mental activities; the five omnipresent factors (*kun 'gro*) are feeling (*tshor ba*), discrimination ('*du shes*), intention (*sems pa*), contact (*reg pa*), and attention (*yid la byed pa*).

The five determining factors (*yul nges*) are aspiration ('*dun pa*), belief (*mos pa*), mindfulness (*dran pa*), stabilization (*ting nge 'dzin*), and knowledge (*shes rab*).

The eleven virtuous mental factors (*dge ba*) are faith (*dad pa*), self-respect (*ngo tsha shes pa*), decency (*khrel yod*), non-attachment (*ma chags pa*), non-hatred (*zhe sdang med pa*), non-confusion (*gti mug med pa*), effort (*brtson 'grus*), mental pliancy (*shin tu sbyangs ba*), conscientiousness (*bag yod*), equanimity (*btang snyoms*), and nonviolence (*rnam par mi 'tshe ba*).

The six basic disturbing attitudes (*rtsa nyon*) are desire (*'dod chags*), anger (*khong khro*), pride (*nga rgyal*), ignorance (*ma rig pa*), doubt (*the tshom*), and deluded views (*lta ba nyon mongs can*).

The twenty secondary disturbing attitudes (*nye nyon*) are aggression (*khro ba*), resentment (*'khon 'dzin*), concealment (*'chab pa*), spite (*'tshig pa*), jealousy (*phrag dog*), miserliness (*ser sna*), deceit (*sgyu*), dissimulation (*g.yo*), inflation (*rgyags pa*), violence (*rnam par 'tshe ba*), lack of self-respect (*ngo tsha med pa*), inconsideration (*khrel med pa*), lethargy (*rmugs pa*), excitement (*rgod pa*), lack of faith (*ma dad pa*), laziness (*le lo*), lack of conscientiousness (*bag med pa*), forgetfulness (*brjed nges pa*), lack of alertness (*shes bzhin med pa*), and distraction (*rnam par g.yeng ba*).

The four changeable factors (*gzhan 'gyur*), which may be positive or negative, are sleep (*gnyid*), regret (*'gyod pa*), investigation (*rtog pa*), and analysis (*dpyod pa*).

41. Foe destroyers (*dgra bcom pa*) are those who have freed themselves from cyclic existence by overcoming our principal foe—the disturbing attitudes and emotions and their seeds. They have conquered the demonic forces of the contaminated aggregates (*phung po'i bdud*), the disturbing emotions (*nyon mongs pa'i bdud*), uncontrolled death (*'chi bdag gi bdud*) and the son of the gods (*lha'i bu yi bdud*). The latter refers to all the obstacles that arise in the course of practice to prevent us getting rid of the former three.

42. Causal motivating ignorance: *rgyu'i kun slong gyur pa'i ma rig pa;* contemporaneous motivating ignorance: *dus kyi kun slong gyur pa'i ma rig pa.*

43. The ignorance accompanying the disturbing emotions is often referred to as *rmongs pa.* If it were a misconception of the self, the desire or hostility it accompanies would necessarily also be such a misconception because they would share five congruent factors (*mtshungs ldan lnga*): similar basis (*rten*) because of depending on the same faculty; similar object (*dmigs pa*) because of sharing the same focal object; similar aspect (*rnam pa*) because the focal object appears to both; similar time (*dus*) because of being simultaneous; similar substance (*rdzas*) because, for instance, one moment of mind can be accompanied by only one feeling.

44. Chapter 7, verse 14, from *The Way of the Bodhisattva,* translated by the Padmakara Translation Group (Boston: Shambhala Publications, 1997).

45. We are free from eight adverse conditions. Four of these are nonhuman states as hell-beings, animals, hungry ghosts, and celestial beings with extremely long lives. The suffering of those in the bad states of rebirth is so intense that they cannot think about spiritual practice. Celestial beings with long lives are absorbed in sensual pleasures or the pleasure of concentration and cannot develop an aversion to cyclic existence. Their bodies and minds are not suitable as a basis for vows of any kind.

There are four human states which prevent authentic practice of the Buddha's teachings, the most serious of which is holding wrong views such as that there are no past and future lives and that there is no connection between actions and their effects. Being born a barbarian in a remote place where there is no access to Buddhist teachings, being born at a time when a Buddha's teachings do not exist in the world, and having defective faculties are also serious impediments. Fortune means enjoying conducive conditions. Five kinds of such fortune are personal: being born as a human; being born in a place where the teachings exist and there are ordained men and women; possessing healthy faculties; not having created any seriously negative actions like the five extremely grave and the five almost as grave actions; and having faith in spiritual teachers, the three kinds of training, and the texts which contain instructions on them. Five kinds of good fortune are circumstantial: that a Buddha has come to the world; that he has lit the lamp of the teachings; that these teachings are alive insofar as there are people who hear, think about, and meditate on them; that there are those who can be looked upon as role models because of their exemplary practice of the teachings; and that support and encouragement for practitioners are available.

46. The eight assets that are a maturation of past actions (*rnam smin gyi yon tan brgyad*): a long life (*tshe ring ba*) through protecting the lives of others; a good appearance (*gzugs bzang ba*) through making offerings, such as lighting butterlamps, to representations of the Three Jewels; belonging to a good family (*rigs mtho ba*) through having respect for others, as though we were their servants; outstanding authority and wealth (*dbang phyug phun sum tshogs pa*) through making effort to be generous; honorable speech (*tshig btsun pa*) that is trusted by others, through speaking circumspectly; great power (*dbang che ba*) through making prayers of aspiration to possess many different good qualities; a strong body and mind (*lus sems stobs dang ldan pa*) through doing heavy work or difficult tasks that others cannot do and that are appropriate for us to do; and being male

(*skye ba nyid yin pa*) through seeing the disadvantages of being female. Though this last point may appear to be outdated, in many societies women are still oppressed and do not enjoy the freedoms we take for granted. In all societies women experience more or less severe difficulties associated with menstruation, childbirth, and menopause, which can prevent them from doing what they wish.

The seven distinguishing attributes or qualities associated with a good rebirth, referred to as high status (*mtho ris kyi yon tan bdun*), bear similarities to the eight assets: to be a member of a good caste or family (*rigs bzang ba*); to have a beautiful appearance or physique (*gzugs mdzes pa*), riches (*sbyor ba* or *nor phyug pa*), authority and wealth (*dbang phyug*), great intelligence (*shes rab che ba*), a long life (*tshe ring ba*), and freedom from sickness (*nad med pa*). An alternative enumeration includes good fortune (*skal ba bzang ba*) instead of authority and wealth.

The four wheels (*'khor lo bzhi*): to live in a conducive place (*mthun pa'i yul na gnas pa*); to rely on a holy being (*skye bu dam pa la brten pa*); to have made prayers of aspiration (*smon lam btab pa*); and to have created a store of merit (*bsod nams bsags pa*).

47. Of the ten harmful activities or nonvirtues (*mi dge ba bcu*)—killing, stealing, sexual misconduct, lying, harsh speech, divisive speech, meaningless speech, covetous thoughts, harmful thoughts, and wrong views—the first seven, activities of body and speech, are considered to be action (*las*). They are also referred to as paths of action (*las kyi lam*) and termed intended action (*bsam pa'i las*). The last three, activities of mind, are not action but the basis with which intention engages (*sems pa 'jug pa'i gzhi*) and are paths of action (*las kyi lam*). Covetousness and harmfulness are disturbing emotions and not action. Mental action (*yid kyi las*)

is the act of intention (*sems pa'i las*), which constitutes the mental factor intention (*sems pa*).

48. The eye source: *mig gi skye mched;* the ear source: *rna ba'i skye mched;* the nose source: *sna'i skye mched;* the tongue source: *lce'i skye mched;* the body or tactile source: *lus kyi skye mched;* the mental source: *yid kyi skye mched.*

49. Either three or four conditions are presented as giving rise to a moment of consciousness. They are the focal condition (*dmigs rkyen*), the main condition (*bdag rkyen*), the immediately preceding condition (*de ma thag rkyen*), and the causal conditions (*rgyu rkyen*), which include these three as well as all other contributing factors. Attention (*yid la byed pa*) is one of the five mental factors that are present with every moment of awareness (*kun 'gro*). Although contact is also one of the omnipresent mental factors, in the context of the twelve links it refers only to contact that occurs in the womb after all six sources have developed.

50. Experience of the object: *yul nyams su myong ba*; experience of maturation: *rnam smin nyams su myong ba.*

51. Experiencer: *longs spyod pa po.*

52. Craving (*sred pa*) here has the same meaning as desire and attachment (*'dod chags*).

53. The principal kind of craving experienced in the desire realm is for the objects of the five senses (*'dod sred*). The craving that manifests in the form and formless realms is referred to as craving for worldly existence (*srid sred*). This is attachment to the different states of absorption that are experienced in these realms and that may be mistaken for

freedom from cyclic existence, although, in fact, they are still part of it. To emphasize this error this is called craving for worldly existence.

54. Grasping at what is desired (*'dod pa nyer bar len pa*); grasping at views (*lta ba nyer bar len pa*), which include extreme views (*mthar lta*), wrong views (*log lta*), and holding false views as supreme (*lta ba mchog 'dzin*); grasping at ethics and discipline (*tshul khrims dang brtul zhugs nyer bar len pa*) and holding these as supreme; and grasping at assertions of a self (*bdag tu smra ba nyer bar len pa*).

55. The most powerful positive or negative imprint will be triggered first. For a detailed explanation of how we create powerful imprints see Je Tsongkhapa's *Great Treatise on the Stages of the Path* (*Lam rim chen mo*) in the section "The Varieties of Karma: A brief discussion of the criteria for powerful actions." If the positive or negative imprints are equally powerful, the imprint of an action with which we have had great familiarity and which we have performed repeatedly will be activated. If there is no difference where familiarity is concerned, the imprint of an action created before others will become active first.

56. Existence: *srid pa*; cyclic existence: *'khor ba*; intermediate existence: *bar srid*; existence at birth: *skye srid*; preparatory existence: *mngon dus kyi srid pa*; existence at death: *'chi srid*.

57. Actions concordant with liberation: *thar pa cha mthun gyi las*.

58. Bodhisattvas insure that their actions are characterized by six excellent features (*dam pa drug*). Whatever they do

has an excellent basis (*rten dam pa*) because they are motivated by the wish to gain enlightenment so as to help others in the most effective way. Their actions are performed with the excellent objective (*ched du bya ba dam pa*) of impartially helping all living beings to find temporary and ultimate happiness. All that they do is intended as an excellent purification (*dag pa dam pa*) of the obstructions to liberation and omniscience by counteracting them. They always use the excellent means (*thabs dam pa*) of understanding emptiness. In each activity the excellent conduct (*spyod pa dam pa*) of incorporating all the perfections is present, and they conclude with the excellent dedication (*bsngo ba*) of the merit they create to the happiness and unsurpassable enlightenment of all living beings.

59. See Appendix 1 for an overview of the contents of Nagarjuna's *Treatise on the Middle Way*.

60. Bimbisara was the king of Magadha at the time of the Buddha Shakyamuni. Bodhgaya, where the Buddha manifested the deed of attaining enlightenment, was situated in his kingdom. At the age of thirty Bimbisara heard the Buddha teach and became his devoted follower. He presented the bamboo grove of Venuvana to the Buddha, who then often taught his followers there. Bimbisara was later murdered by his son Ajatashatru.

61. The state of a stream enterer (*rgyun zhugs 'bras gnas*) is a stage of attainment associated with the Lesser Vehicle, whose practices lead to personal liberation from cyclic existence. There are four states of approaching (*zhugs pa*) certain fruits of practice and four states of abiding in those fruits (*'bras gnas*).

There are five factors that accord with the lowest of the

three realms of existence (*tha ma'i cha mthun lnga*): the false
view of the transitory collection (*'jig tshogs la lta ba*), holding misleading forms of discipline and conduct as supreme
(*tshul khrims dang brtul zhugs mchog 'dzin*), desire for objects of the senses (*'dod pa la 'dun pa*), doubt (*the tshom*)
and harmful thoughts (*gnod sems*). Of the three realms—the
desire, form and formless realms—the desire realm is the
lowest. These five factors accord with the desire realm because the third and the fifth prevent one from taking rebirth
beyond the desire realm. While one still harbors the other
three, one may take birth in one of the higher realms but
must eventually be reborn in the desire realm again.

Those who are approaching the fruit of a stream enterer
are primarily engaged in freeing themselves from the three
fetters: the intellectually formed false view of the transitory
collection (*'jig tshogs la lta ba kun btags*) as a real "I" and
"mine," holding misleading forms of discipline and conduct
as supreme, and deluded doubt. The three fetters are singled
out as major hindrances to the attainment of liberation. Respectively they are compared to not wanting to set out on a
journey, taking a wrong road, and being in doubt about what
road to follow. When one has freed oneself from these fetters, one abides in the fruit of a stream enterer.

Practitioners who are engaged in ridding themselves
of most of the above-mentioned five factors are approaching the fruit of a once returner (*phyir 'ong zhugs pa*) and
those who have succeeded in doing so abide in the fruit of
a once returner (*phyir 'ong 'bras gnas*). This means that
they will take birth in the desire realm once or twice more
as a result of actions underlain by disturbing attitudes and
emotions.

Practitioners who are engaged in getting rid of all of these
factors are approaching the fruit of a never returner (*phyir mi
'ong zhugs pa*), while those who have succeeded abide in the

fruit of a never returner (*phyir mi 'ong 'bras gnas*) and will never again take birth in the desire realm.

There are five factors which accord with the upper realms (*gong ma'i cha mthun lnga*): desire belonging to the form and formless realms (*gzugs dang gzugs med las skyes pa'i 'dod chags*), excitement (*rgod pa*), pride (*nga rgyal*) and ignorance (*ma rig pa*). These prevent one from going beyond the upper realms of cyclic existence. Practitioners who are endeavoring to rid themselves of these five factors are approaching the state of a foe destroyer (*dgra bcom zhugs pa*) and those who have succeeded abide in the fruit of a foe destroyer (*dgra bcom 'bras gnas*).

62. *Samādhirājasūtra, Ting nge 'dzin rgyal po'i mdo*, P795, Vol. 31-32.

63. *dBu ma rtsa ba'i tshig le'ur byas pa shes rab ces bya ba'i rnam bshad rigs pa'i rgya mtsho*, commonly known as *rTsa she Ṭik chen*, P6153, Vol. 156. English translation: rJe Tsong khapa, *Ocean of Reasoning: A Great Commentary on Nāgārjuna's Mūlamadhyamakakārikā*, trans. Geshe Ngawang Samten and Jay L. Garfield (New York: Oxford University Press, 2006).

64. The afflicted side: *kun nas nyon mongs pa'i phyogs*; the purified side: *rnam par byang ba'i phyogs*. True suffering and true causes of suffering belong to the former; true cessation and true paths of insight, to the latter.

SOURCE READINGS

Commentaries in Tibetan that served as a basis for this teaching:

Zab mo rten cing 'brel bar 'byung ba'i mtha' dpyod legs par bshad pa'i rgya mtsho by Sras Ngag dbang bkra shis (1678-1738)

dBu ma rtsa ba'i tshig le'ur byas pa shes rab ces bya ba'i rnam bshad rigs pa'i rgya mtsho by Tsong kha pa Blo bzang grags pa (1357-1419)

rTen 'brel gyi thal 'phreng mkhas pa'i mgul rgyan by rJe btsun Chos kyi rgyal mtshan (1469-1544)